"In this beautiful[l]
Amy Ekeh shows
to us and offer hea
those seeking to pray with the Scriptures."

—Frank J. Matera, professor emeritus,
The Catholic University of America

"Amy Ekeh's reflections, as usual, enrich our reading of the
Gospel stories in such wonderful and often surprising ways.
Praying with this beautiful book will help us become ever
better healers and allow ourselves to be healed."

—Carol Keehan, DC, retired president/CEO,
Catholic Health Association

"Amy Ekeh has mined profound insights from each Gospel
story that will surely guide healing encounters with the Lord in
personal prayer, pastoral care, homiletics, and faith formation."

—Bruce T. Morrill, SJ, author of *Divine Worship
and Human Healing*

"These reflections will serve homilists, caregivers, and anyone
who's ever longed, deeply and personally, for the healing touch
of Jesus."

—Alice Camille, author of *For Everything There Is a Season*
and *A Little Book of Light*

"This beautiful work will bring hope to so many in our broken world who seek the healing touch of Christ. Amy Ekeh has given us a treasure: an insightful, thought-provoking, soul-stirring look at the stories of healing in the Gospels that ends up being a kind of ongoing, heartfelt prayer."

—Deacon Greg Kandra, journalist and author of
    A Deacon Prays

"Amy Ekeh has succeeded in packing into one book an astonishing amount of colloquial, meaty, thought-provoking reflection on the healing stories of the Gospels."

—Genevieve Glen, OSB, author of *Sauntering through
    Scripture* and *By Lamplight*

"*Stretch Out Your Hand* is a delightful book on the healing ministry of Jesus filled with fresh spiritual and biblical insights. If you or your loved ones are in need of healing, this book is definitely for you."

—vănThanh Nguyễn, SVD, professor of New Testament
    studies, Catholic Theological Union

Stretch Out Your Hand

*Reflections on the Healing
Ministry of Jesus*

Amy Ekeh

Introduction by Thomas D. Stegman, SJ

LITURGICAL PRESS
Collegeville, Minnesota

litpress.org

Cover art: *Go On, Thomas* by Jack Baumgartner

Library of Congress Cataloging-in-Publication Data

Names: Ekeh, Amy, author.
Title: Stretch out your hand : reflections on the healing ministry of
    Jesus / Amy Ekeh ; introduction by Thomas D. Stegman, SJ.
Description: Collegeville, Minnesota : Liturgical Press, [2025] |
    Includes bibliographical references. | Summary: "These forty
    reflections take us deep into the heart of powerful Gospel stories,
    helping us hear and experience them anew so we too may stretch
    out our hands-to receive and to extend the healing ministry of
    Jesus"— Provided by publisher.
Identifiers: LCCN 2024028618 (print) | LCCN 2024028619 (ebook)
    | ISBN 9780814669815 (trade paperback) | ISBN 9780814669822
    (epub) | ISBN 9780814689660 (pdf)
Subjects: LCSH: Spiritual healing—Christianity. | Healing—Religious
    aspects—Christianity. | Bible. Gospels.
Classification: LCC BT732.5 .E39 2025 (print) | LCC BT732.5 (ebook)
    | DDC 234/.131—dc23/eng/20240807
LC record available at https://lccn.loc.gov/2024028618
LC ebook record available at https://lccn.loc.gov/2024028619

For Tom

May I find my healing in this giving.

—*Prayer of Surrender of Fr. Walter Ciszek, SJ*

Contents

Preface

The Desire for Healing

The desire for healing is an instinct that binds us all—a feeling that "all is not right," a yearning for transformation, an urge to live freely beyond the limits of our fragility. Into this human desire comes a God whose love extends to every person, a Redeemer whose touch brings the wholeness we long for, a Spirit whose presence is balm spilling over into every corner of our hearts and lives.

Yes, in our desire to be healed, we are blessed. Not because the yearning stops. Not because the questions are answered or the cures guaranteed. We are blessed because this path we walk is one of promise: our God is a God who heals.

This book on Jesus' healing ministry was originally envisioned as a joint project with Thomas D. Stegman, SJ. It was our shared wish to spend time with these extraordinary Gospel stories, to imagine and pray with them, to write about them, perhaps even to bring some comfort to those who deeply yearn for the restorative touch of this healer from Nazareth. The idea was conceived in the midst of

Tom's own struggle with a terminal diagnosis of glioblastoma. Until very close to the end of his life, it was his firm intention to write this book. (We did get as far as a joint introduction, which you will find below.)

In one of our conversations about this project, Tom told me he wanted to explore one idea in particular: the distinction between *being cured* and *being healed*. He knew that without a miracle—for which many fervently prayed—a cure was not in his future. And yet, *healing . . .* this was something he lived and breathed. The belief that the healing hand of Jesus Christ was firmly grasping his own was enough. And he willingly extended that hand to others, a healing presence in his own right.

Ever the teacher, Tom died on Holy Saturday—April 8, 2023. And so the writing of this book falls to me alone. But I do it in his friendship, believing he is with the Living One, and honoring his belief that one need not be cured in order to be healed, and that the human desire for wholeness is nothing other than our invitation to God to come and change us.

Amy Ekeh

Thomas D. Stegman, SJ (1963–2023), was dean and professor of New Testament at the Boston College Clough School of Theology and Ministry—a respected scholar, prolific author, and popular retreat director. A Jesuit of the Midwest Province of the Society of Jesus, Tom was also a beloved brother, son, and uncle; a valued colleague; and a friend to many.

Introduction

Fr. Tom Stegman's original introduction is below.

As I type these words during a gentle snowfall in New England, I have two lines from today's eucharistic liturgy ringing in my ears. One is the verse from the Gospel Acclamation: "Jesus preached the gospel of the kingdom and cured every disease among the people" (Matt 4:23). The other is Jesus' response in the Gospel reading to the poignant cry of a leper that, if the Lord wished, the man would be made clean. Jesus' response? He was "moved with pity" or, better, "moved with compassion" (Mark 1:41). And out of that compassion, Jesus touched the man and healed him.

We can glean two important ideas from these lines that will help to set the stage for the reflections that follow. First, there is an inextricable link between Jesus' healing ministry and his proclamation of the coming of the reign of God. Jesus, who came to inaugurate God's reign, does so in no small part by healing people of various illnesses and afflictions. In doing so, he shows that God's design for God's people is that they experience wholeness and fullness of life. As the evangelist John expresses it, Jesus came to reveal God's love (3:16), through which we might "have life, and have it abundantly" (10:10).

Second, the Gospel verses quoted above make clear that Jesus' healing ministry is a manifestation of God's *compassion* for us. Our God is no distant "unmoved mover" but one who cares deeply for all creatures. Jesus is the face of God's love and compassion. His healings reveal not only God's salvific power but also the attribute that gives rise to this power—namely, divine compassion.

Another line from the Gospels bears mention. (It happens to be a favorite of my friend and co-author, Amy Ekeh.) Jesus commands a man whose hand is crippled: "Stretch out your hand" (Mark 3:5). The man does so, and immediately his hand is restored. This account illustrates that Jesus, in his healing ministry, upholds the dignity and agency of those to whom he ministers. The man in need of healing was active, not passive, in the healing process. This empowerment, this engagement, is another manifestation of Jesus' healing work.

It is our hope that this book will enrich your encounter with these Gospel texts and, more importantly, assist you in receiving their healing effects.

Tom Stegman, SJ
Weston, Massachusetts

As I type these words, the sun is setting behind the stand of trees outside my window. This is the time of day when "all those who had any who were sick . . . brought them to [Jesus]; and he laid his hands on each of them and cured them" (Luke 4:40). This is the time of day when the compassion of Jesus reached the multitudes, when the people knew that the touch of his outstretched hand would change their lives forever. Who knows how many evenings they gathered around him as the sun set behind the trees? Who knows how many he touched, how untiring his compassion, as evening fell?

The healing ministry of Jesus is a rich and complex area for spiritual exploration. As we immerse ourselves in these stories—the rawness of exorcisms, the desperation of parents with sick children, the astonishing faith of the vulnerable— we may find ourselves changing right alongside those who are healed. Questions and doubts that have plagued us for years may give way to the fundamental reality of encounter with God. Our intense desire for healing, for the connections that make us whole, may find renewed hope in the sound of Jesus' voice and the touch of his hand. Our hesitation to call out, our unwillingness to admit before all that we too are vulnerable, may finally find a voice as Jesus passes by. Then we will be ready to sit at the roadside with Bartimaeus and shout from the depths of our being, "Jesus, Son of David, have mercy on me!" (Mark 10:47). And we too will be healed.

Amy Ekeh
Milford, Connecticut

Reading the Healing Stories

In addition to offering reflections on Jesus' healing ministry, this book also serves as a collection of the healing stories of the Gospels. Almost all of them are included here for your prayerful reflection.

As with any Gospel text, we come to these stories with some familiarity. We know the stories of Jesus and the people he encountered. And yet, the living Word always has something new to reveal to us. As you read these beautiful texts of encounter and accompaniment, strive with all your heart to read them as if for the first time. Let the smallest details sink in, let the images linger in your mind, let the people come to life. Meet their eyes and hear their voices. Look at the healer from Nazareth as though you've never seen him before. Breathe the stories! And let them breathe in you.

The Gospel accounts in this book generally follow the timeline of Jesus' ministry, from his earliest proclamation of the kingdom of God to his arrest in the Garden of Gethsemane. They are taken from all four Gospels, but you will notice that many of them come from the Gospel of Mark. This is because when the same story is told by Matthew, Mark, and Luke, it is Mark that often gives us the most detailed account. And for our own imagining and reflecting, as we will see, these details are of tremendous value.

You'll find that several stories have more than one reflection connected with them. In these cases, we'll explore several facets of a single healing story.

For groups that are reading these reflections and discussing them together, you may wish to begin your discussions by sharing with one another your own reflections on the Gospel stories themselves. You will be amazed by what each of you notices, how others in your group speak about these stories, and what insights you generate together.

May Jesus the Healer grasp us by the hand as together we set out to explore his extraordinary healing ministry.

Reflections

Jesus Heals at Sunset

Luke 4:40

[40] As the sun was setting, all those who had any who were sick with various kinds of diseases brought them to him; and he laid his hands on each of them and cured them.

1

At Sunset

A beautiful scene in a single verse, Luke's image of Jesus healing at sunset in Capernaum takes our breath away. To have been there! But there is so much we can imagine.

First, the sick, those with "various kinds of diseases." For many of them, travel was hard. Some were in pain. Some were exhausted. But all of them were hoping.

Second, the loved ones of the sick, those who "brought them to him." If you have ever watched someone suffer, you know the stress and strain, the worry they carried with them. And you know the hope with which they came. Who knows how many miles they walked with their sick, to bring them to the healer from Nazareth?

Third, the sheer numbers! In Mark's version of this scene, he remarks that "the whole city was gathered around the door" of the house where Jesus was (1:33). *The whole city*? The desire for healing is strong.

Finally, Jesus. One doesn't suppose that Jesus had been sitting idle all day. So he must have been tired. But he didn't turn away; he didn't stop. No, one by one he touched "each of them." We can only imagine the compassion that served as counterpoint to the hope of the people. Compassion that came from a well so deep that it gave no thought on this night to the numbers awaiting him in the next town—and the next, and the next. Compassion that knew no discouragement. Compassion that touched every single one.

It was sunset. The time of day when things begin to quiet down, when we are reminded of the rhythms of night and day, when we recall that an end does come and the light does not last forever. But across the sky are colors, beautiful colors. Across the hearts of the people, hope. Upon the mind of Jesus, love.

He laid his hands on each of them and cured them.

Meditation: The physical, created world can be a place of suffering, but it is also a place of profound compassion. Let the next sunset you see remind you of this scene from Luke's Gospel. Imagine yourself in the presence of Jesus as day gives way to night.

Prayer: Jesus, as the sun sets on this day, remind me of your tireless compassion, your willingness to touch me, your refusal to ever stop healing.

The Kingdom of God Has Come Near

Mark 1:14-15

[14]Jesus came to Galilee, proclaiming the good news of God, [15]and saying, "The time is fulfilled, and the kingdom of God has come near; repent, and believe in the good news."

2

Start at the Beginning

Fr. Frank Matera, longtime professor of New Testament at The Catholic University of America, was known for giving this assignment to new students of the Gospels:

1. Find some time and a quiet place to sit.
2. Forget everything you think you know about Jesus.
3. Read the Gospel of Mark from beginning to end.

I still remember exactly where I sat. I remember the quiet, the "forgetting," the reading of Mark's Gospel as though for the first time.

The experience was nothing short of shocking. It was exciting, eye-opening, transformative. As I took in the entire Gospel in one sitting, it filled my imagination in a way it never had in bits and pieces. And the Jesus I met—he was not like the Jesus I had always known. He was grittier, more demanding, unflinching, driven. Everything he did and said expressed urgency. His mission was not to inspire or to comfort. It was, to borrow a phrase from another Gospel, to light a fire on the earth—and to light it *now* (Luke 12:49).

Mark's Gospel was likely the earliest Gospel written, so it makes sense that it presents us with the rawest portrait of Jesus. While later Gospels tend to present Jesus as a bit more "above the fray," Mark doesn't shy away from realities like Jesus' anger, his physical hunger, his compassion so deep it was almost visceral. One of my students described Jesus in Mark's Gospel with the old Latin phrase *Veni, vidi, vici:* "I came, I saw, I conquered."

Jesus' mission in Mark is crystal clear. He came for one reason: to preach the good news of the kingdom of God (1:38). And preach he did, with words and with living. Indeed, after reminding his disciples that his purpose was to "proclaim the message," he was approached by a man with leprosy—kneeling, begging—and Jesus stretched out his hand. The healing, like almost everything in this fast-paced Gospel, is immediate.

When reflecting on the healing ministry of Jesus, we are best off starting at the beginning. And the beginning is the proclamation of the good news of God. Jesus embodied that message—one of urgent expectation and from-the-gut compassion, a message calling for the transformation of every hearer, the kind from which there is no going back.

The kingdom of God has come near. The fire is burning.

Meditation: Our response to the urgent proclamation of Jesus is faith. To respond in faith often requires a change of heart—thus Jesus' call to "repent." Repentance is not a guilty feeling. It is better understood as a change of direction. This change may be an emerging openness to the miraculous or a fresh resolve to believe that we deserve to be healed, to believe that the compassion of Jesus could actually be directed toward us.

Prayer: Jesus, you proclaimed a new way of life. To live it, I must be healed and whole. Grant me the grace of repentance, so I may let you change me.

Jesus Heals a Man with an Unclean Spirit

Mark 1:21-26

²¹They went to Capernaum; and when the sabbath came, he entered the synagogue and taught. ²²They were astounded at his teaching, for he taught them as one having authority, and not as the scribes. ²³Just then there was in their synagogue a man with an unclean spirit, ²⁴and he cried out, "What have you to do with us, Jesus of Nazareth? Have you come to destroy us? I know who you are, the Holy One of God." ²⁵But Jesus rebuked him, saying, "Be silent, and come out of him!" ²⁶And the unclean spirit, convulsing him and crying with a loud voice, came out of him.

3

The Holy One of God

Mark's Gospel is known for its graphic scenes and vivid detail. This story from the earliest days of Jesus' public ministry is an excellent example. We can almost imagine ourselves there in the synagogue. It's a terrifying scene.

The story begins with an affirmation of Jesus' authority, which should prepare us for what follows. But it doesn't. I don't know that we can ever be prepared for evil.

It happens suddenly ("Just then," a translation of one of Mark's favorite Greek words, *euthys*, which means "immediately"). *Just then*, evil speaks. More accurately, evil "cries out." The unclean spirit addresses Jesus with two names: "Jesus of Nazareth" and "Holy One of God." One is personal—the name given to him by his parents, the place where he grew up. The second shocks even the reader, coming as it does so early in Mark's Gospel. Evil knows Jesus not only as a man but as God's own representative—sacred, set apart, holy, unique.

The spirit fears one thing—the same thing we all fear—death. Ceasing to exist. "Have you come to destroy us?" the spirit asks the Holy One.

In her book *Signs and Wonders*, Amy-Jill Levine notes that while on some level healing stories may comfort us, on a deeper level they make us nervous. I would venture to say they may even disturb us greatly. This is because healers put their fingers on evil. They literally touch it.

This is not a battle evil can win. And yet, the scene still sends a chill down our spines. We have seen, perhaps even felt, the unclean spirit of illness or brokenness. It does indeed cry out. It resists defeat. We are convulsed by it!

Praise God that Jesus of Nazareth is the Holy One. Praise God that his authority calls forth and silences even what shakes us to our core.

Meditation: Jesus' words make it clear that he perceives two distinct beings before him: *the man* and *the unclean spirit*. Jesus says: "Be silent [unclean spirit], and come out of him [the man]!" Is there any area of your life where you feel that evil is creeping in, influencing you to be someone other than your true self? Is jealousy, resentment, anger, or pain controlling you in a way that feels invasive? Jesus has authority. Ask him to intervene.

Prayer: Jesus, Healer, cast out everything unclean in me.

Jesus Heals the Royal Official's Son

John 4:46-53

[46]Now there was a royal official whose son lay ill in Capernaum. [47]When he heard that Jesus had come from Judea to Galilee, he went and begged him to come down and heal his son, for he was at the point of death. [48]Then Jesus said to him, "Unless you see signs and wonders you will not believe." [49]The official said to him, "Sir, come down before my little boy dies." [50]Jesus said to him, "Go; your son will live." The man believed the word that Jesus spoke to him and started on his way. [51]As he was going down, his slaves met him and told him that his child was alive. [52]So he asked them the hour when he began to recover, and they said to him, "Yesterday at one in the afternoon the fever left him." [53]The father realized that this was the hour when Jesus had said to him, "Your son will live." So he himself believed, along with his whole household.

4

Those Who Beg

The royal official in John's Gospel is often recognized for his faith in Jesus. And his faith is admirable. But I notice him for begging.

He went and begged Jesus to come down and heal his son. We find references to "begging" scattered throughout the Gospels, not infrequently in healing stories: parents begging for the health of their children, people begging for the restoration of sight or the ability to walk. These are not small requests.

The idea of begging may sound repulsive to us, even pathetic. People who beg seem to lack self-respect. They have lost their dignity. They are out of control.

But those who beg are really models for the rest of us. They have experienced pain so deep that they are far beyond worrying about their image or self-respect or what others might say. They are far beyond caring about how dirty their clothes will be if they kneel in the dirt or fall to the ground in front of Jesus. They are far beyond any illusion that they are in control. This kind of pain, though not something that we would ever want, is likely to come to us. It can be helpful to read about it first, on the sacred page.

Second, those who beg in the Gospels are direct and authentic. They aren't tentative. They don't hesitate or hold back. They are gut-wrenchingly honest and astonishingly trusting. Pain has eradicated every last ounce of inhibition. They are completely and utterly vulnerable.

It is this outright vulnerability that I find most beautiful, most redeeming, in these stories. I don't believe God ever purposefully inflicts illness or pain on us, yet they are part of our existence. And so often these are the experiences that strip away our illusions and our facades. We won't change if we aren't vulnerable.

As it turns out, begging isn't weak—it's bold. Boldness and vulnerability go hand in hand. May we be so bold as to beg. May we be so vulnerable as to be changed.

Meditation: Have you ever begged God for something? What circumstances brought you there? Did you feel out of control, or completely free, or both? If you don't recall a time when you've prayed so earnestly, have you ever been close? What held you back? Were you afraid of the emotions that might come with such a vulnerable way of praying? The desire, the request, is already in your heart. Give it to God with total abandon.

Prayer: Jesus—without embarrassment, without pretense, without hesitation—I beg you to bring healing into my life. Change me in the ways I need most—body, mind, soul, and spirit.

Jesus Heals Simon's Mother-in-Law

Mark 1:29-31

29 As soon as they left the synagogue, they entered the house of Simon and Andrew, with James and John. 30 Now Simon's mother-in-law was in bed with a fever, and they told him about her at once. 31 He came and took her by the hand and lifted her up. Then the fever left her, and she began to serve them.

5

Egeiro

Three actions of Jesus are the centerpiece of this short healing story, but they are flanked by the actions of others. Prompting the healing is the urgent concern of those in the house for Simon's mother-in-law ("they told him about her at once"). And following the healing is the incredible, immediate act of service on the part of the healed woman ("she began to serve"). One might think she would take a bit of time to herself first! But she does not.

The healing itself comes about through these three actions of Jesus: *He came . . . took her by the hand . . . lifted her up.*

He came. It's easy to miss this part of the healing, but it is essential to the person of Jesus. When people ask for him, he comes. Being present is what he does. We can think of instances where Jesus delayed (John 11:6) or where he healed from afar (Matt 8:13). But those stories are not typical. He usually healed by being physically present.

He took her by the hand. The touch of Jesus' hand—or others reaching out to Jesus with their hands—is pervasive in the healing stories of the Gospels. This physical imagery is vivid; it resonates with us. Our hands are familiar, powerful tools of connection. And in this story, Jesus grasping the hand of Simon's mother-in-law in his own is the beginning of healing.

He lifted her up. The Greek verb used here is *egeiro*, meaning "to awaken" or "to raise up." The same root word is spoken by Jesus to the man who was paralyzed ("rise" or "stand up"; Mark 2:11) and to the young girl he raises from the dead ("arise" or "get up"; Mark 5:41). Most importantly, it is the same verb used by a young man in a white robe, sitting on the right side of the empty tomb of Jesus: "He has been raised; he is not here" (Mark 16:6).

The lifting up, the standing on her own two feet, of Simon's mother-in-law is nothing short of a foreshadowing of the resurrection of Jesus. Something amiss has been set right. Something laid low has been raised up.

In fact, every healing is a foreshadowing of the resurrection of Jesus. And every healing is a resurrection in its own right. The grasp of the healer's outstretched hand awakens and lifts up. Angels announce that the dead are living—and no longer present in the old places like beds and tombs—for they are out and about, serving and proclaiming that God is about life and *egeiro*—rising.

Meditation: Scripture includes many references to the hand of God. It is God's hand that creates (Isa 45:12), delivers Israel from oppression in Egypt (Exod 7:5), and reaches out "all day long," even to a rebellious people (Isa 65:2). It is this hand of God that continues to reach out in the person of Jesus—to create, to liberate, to extend love, patience, and healing, no matter how long or how often we rebel.

Prayer: Come, Lord Jesus. Take me by the hand and raise me up.

Jesus Heals a Man with a Skin Disease

Mark 1:40-42

[40]A leper came to him begging him, and kneeling he said to him, "If you choose, you can make me clean." [41]Moved with pity, Jesus stretched out his hand and touched him, and said to him, "I do choose. Be made clean!" [42]Immediately the leprosy left him, and he was made clean.

6

If You Choose

The initiative of those who seek healing in the Gospels is remarkable. Jesus, though not passive, doesn't tend to take the lead. He takes his cues from those who come to him.

The story of this man with a skin disease is a classic example. *He* takes the initiative—to come, to beg, to kneel, to speak. But most remarkable are his words to Jesus: "If you choose, you can make me clean." A master class in prayer.

If you choose. The opening phrase is a potent combination of total humility and a bit of spiritual arm-twisting. The man knows he is not in control here. His fate is in Jesus' hands. He can ask, and he can ask boldly, but the "if" is a humble handing-over of his situation to Jesus. On the other hand, "If you choose" exerts gentle but real pressure on Jesus. *Here I am,* the man says with his presence, his kneeling stance, his skin disease on full display. *It's up to you what to do about it.*

You can make me clean. It is up to Jesus to decide what to do about the skin disease, but the man has a suggestion.

You don't get the sense that he's losing his nerve, or that his voice is trailing off, or that the look in Jesus' eye discourages him in any way. *You can make me clean*, the man says boldly. *It's up to you.*

He certainly has Jesus' attention. I imagine an intense gaze between the two of them. Mark describes Jesus here, as he does elsewhere, as "moved with pity" or "moved with compassion" (6:34; 8:2; 9:22). The root of the Greek word for "moved with compassion" is *splanchnon*, the human gut—the bowels or intestines, the heart. This man has moved Jesus, deeply.

"I do choose," Jesus responds, stretching out his hand to touch him. The healing action belongs to Jesus, but the initiative belongs to the man before him. The gaze, the touch, the deep-seated compassion—all are *response*. This is the relationship that is prayer.

Meditation: Asking for healing can feel like a risk, but it is one we have to take. And this anonymous man in Mark's Gospel shows us how to do it: by drawing close to Jesus; being utterly, completely, even publicly vulnerable before him; and asking for exactly what is on our minds and hearts. To say "If you choose" isn't really twisting Jesus' arm. Rather, it is recognizing that we need him. It is knowing that he *does* choose, and that even when healing feels long delayed, his hand is stretching toward us.

Prayer: Jesus, if you choose, you can make me clean.

Jesus Forgives a Man Who Is Paralyzed

Mark 2:1-5

¹When he returned to Capernaum after some days, it was reported that he was at home. ²So many gathered around that there was no longer room for them, not even in front of the door; and he was speaking the word to them. ³Then some people came, bringing to him a paralyzed man, carried by four of them. ⁴And when they could not bring him to Jesus because of the crowd, they removed the roof above him; and after having dug through it, they let down the mat on which the paralytic lay. ⁵When Jesus saw their faith, he said to the paralytic, "Son, your sins are forgiven."

7

Faith

Sometimes the Gospels sound as though faith is required for Jesus to heal. In fact, one of the strangest verses in Mark's Gospel seems to indicate that Jesus *couldn't* work miracles if people did not believe. That may upset us, but it is what the Gospel says: "And he *could do no deed of power there* [in Nazareth], except that he laid his hands on a few sick people and cured them. And he was amazed at their unbelief" (6:5-6; emphasis added).

But in other places in the Gospels, Jesus works miracles with the purpose of *bringing about faith* in those who witness them. In other words, faith does not precede miracles but follows them. One of the most dramatic miracles in the Gospels, the raising of Lazarus, is a good example. Before commanding Lazarus to come out of the tomb, amid all the weeping and the concern over the smell of the dead body, Jesus prays (quite loudly, we might imagine): "Father, I thank you for having heard me. I knew that you always hear me, but I have said this for the sake of the crowd standing here, so that they may believe that you sent me" (John 11:41-42). After describing Lazarus's emergence from the tomb and Jesus' command to onlookers to "unbind him," John writes that, having seen these things, many of those who were present "believed in him" (11:44-45).

Does faith bring about miracles, or do miracles bring about faith? Does God expect faith before healing us? Or does healing prompt us toward faith? The answer to all of these questions, of course, is yes. We can no more separate faith and healing than we can separate ourselves and God. There is no hard boundary between the two.

In the story of the man who is paralyzed, whose four friends are bound and determined that he should be touched by Jesus of Nazareth, Mark tells us that Jesus saw with his own eyes the faith of the man's friends. And he responded to it with action. Faith seems to have produced a miracle.

But we might consider the fact that there were four friends. Yes, they acted as one to lower their friend through a hole they dug in the roof (Can you imagine the damage?) to deliver him to Jesus. These friends had faith by the bucketful! And yet . . . is it possible that one of them just really wasn't sure? Is it possible that one of them might have been uncomfortable with such a bold move? Might one have been going through the motions, *wanting* to have faith but not able to muster it, deep in his heart?

Not only possible, I think, but probable. We are human. Faith, even in Jesus of Nazareth, ebbs and flows. What doesn't change is his faith in us.

Meditation: It can be challenging to know ourselves, to know what we truly believe and how firmly we believe it. There may be times when we are surprised by how strong our faith is, and times when we are surprised by its weakness. It might comfort us to know that God expects this. God knows we want to believe and trust. But, as in any relationship, there are ups and downs. Rest easy in the assurance that God understands the human heart. God understands *your* heart.

Prayer: Jesus, you know my heart. You know I believe. Help my unbelief! (Mark 9:24)

8

Friends

Perhaps the most beautiful thing about the healing stories of Jesus is the human interaction within them. Healing is never a solitary process.

In the story of the man who is paralyzed, we know very little about the man's four friends. Actually, there were more than four—the text says that a group of people came, bringing the man to Jesus. But there were four of them who (literally) did the heavy lifting.

These friends were every bit as involved in the healing of this man as Jesus was. Jesus did not sit in his home and blink his eyes and heal people all over the world. He healed people that came to him. He healed people who were brought to him. He healed those he could touch. This man needed to be in the presence of Jesus. That is where the friends come in.

Just typing those words sends a tingle down my spine. Because I know that I too have been completely dependent upon others to bring me into the presence of Jesus. In my own paralysis—whether of apathy, cynicism, confusion, or hardship—it is rare that I have mustered the strength or the wherewithal to drag myself into his healing presence. It is friends—one, four, many—who have so often taken me there. Sometimes these friends have been the obvious candidates—lifelong companions, spiritual mentors, family members. But sometimes they have been unexpected friends—an artist, a colleague, a stranger whose story I read in the news.

This is the power of the human community, a power to heal. This is the power we have to pick each other up and carry one another—no matter how heavy the burden, no matter what obstacles must be overcome—to bring one another into the healing presence of Jesus.

Meditation: Imagine that Jesus is passing by. You need him, but you are unable to move. Who do you see lifting you up and carrying you into his presence?

Prayer: Lord Jesus, bless me with a community that brings me to you.

9

Forgiveness

Is it possible that human beings may gradually be losing the ability to forgive? We seem to be getting better at excusing ourselves from it and worse at actually doing it.

Perhaps the saddest thing about this is that if fewer of us are offering forgiveness, then fewer of us are receiving it. And there is simply nothing like the experience of being forgiven. It is a kind of love that changes us forever. It brings us face-to-face with what is best in others and what is lovable in ourselves. To be forgiven is to be mended. It is to be healed.

This story of the man who is paralyzed, lowered into a house by his friends so Jesus can heal him, says it all. Jesus looked at the man and, as tended to happen when he looked at people, clearly loved him.

And his first inclination? Upon seeing this man—lying on a mat, unable to stand, carried a great distance by his friends, lowered through a dug-out hole, desperate for healing? His inclination was to forgive.

We have no idea what this man's sins were. It doesn't matter. I doubt Jesus cared either. What he cared about was *what this man needed*. And he needed to be forgiven. He needed to be loved and changed. And this was the work Jesus instinctively did. This was the first, and the essential, healing.

Interestingly, Jesus was responding not to the man's faith but to that of his friends (2:5). They too knew what this man needed. Of course, his physical health may have been at the forefront of their minds. They were surely thinking of his family, his livelihood, his personal happiness. But they too knew what he truly needed. A *healing* even more than a curing.

Oh, these friends! They are a sturdy shelter. Whoever finds such a one has found a treasure (Sir 6:14)!

Meditation: Forgiveness has the power to heal relationships. It is never easy to forgive. Sometimes it feels entirely impossible. While God can forgive us in a heartbeat, it usually takes us much longer to forgive someone who has hurt us. But we must keep trying. The forgiveness we offer—even bit by bit, even if it takes years or an entire lifetime—heals us just as much as it heals the one we forgive.

Prayer: Jesus, may your forgiving love heal me so I can heal others. Give me the grace and strength to forgive, and the patience to see the process through.

Jesus Cures a Man Who Is Paralyzed

Mark 2:6-12

[6]Now some of the scribes were sitting there, questioning in their hearts, [7]"Why does this fellow speak in this way? It is blasphemy! Who can forgive sins but God alone?" [8]At once Jesus perceived in his spirit that they were discussing these questions among themselves; and he said to them, "Why do you raise such questions in your hearts? [9]Which is easier, to say to the paralytic, 'Your sins are forgiven,' or to say, 'Stand up and take your mat and walk'? [10]But so that you may know that the Son of Man has authority on earth to forgive sins"—he said to the paralytic— [11]"I say to you, stand up, take your mat and go to your home." [12]And he stood up, and immediately took the mat and went out before all of them; so that they were all amazed and glorified God, saying, "We have never seen anything like this!"

10

Which Is Easier?

A dramatic, total, physical healing follows the forgiveness of the man who is paralyzed. But its drama only serves to highlight the fact that physical healing is secondary.

Surprisingly, the healing doesn't appear to stem directly from Jesus' compassion. As the story is told, it is not as though Jesus was planning all along to forgive the man's sins and then heal his paralysis. In forgiving his sins, Jesus may have felt that the healing was total and effective. Indeed, the physical healing of the paralysis only comes about as a result of the accusations of the scribes, who are depicted as seething in their hearts, questioning Jesus' boldness—his authority, his ability—to declare the forgiveness of sins.

Jesus' initial response, a rhetorical question, has no answer: "Which is easier, to say to the paralytic, 'Your sins are forgiven,' or to say, 'Stand up and take your mat and walk'?" Neither task is easy. Both come about by divine authority, and both are within Jesus' power. He has already done one. Now he has decided to do the other.

Of course, we already know that the two types of healing —one a deep transformation of the human spirit, the other a life-changing physical cure—are connected. In the person of Jesus, whose physical presence embodies the kingdom of God, all that is broken becomes whole, whether of mind, body, or spirit.

And yet, predictably, it is the physical healing that garners the awe of the crowd. After the forgiveness of sins, the room was quiet enough for Jesus to hear the inner rumblings of the hearts of the scribes. But after the physical healing, the crowd responds with awe and glorifies God.

I don't blame them. I can't. We would all do the same. But here is a reminder to each of us that there is a difference between being cured and being healed, and that, in the mind of Jesus, while both are possible, only one is essential.

Meditation: When we or a loved one are in need of physical healing, it is only natural that this need is at the forefront of our minds. And we must not be afraid to desire and believe in and ask for this kind of healing. But we know there will be times when a physical cure does not come. In these times, it can be comforting to know that healing is still possible—the kind of healing that results from presence and love, healing that is essential and eternal, that transforms every thought of our minds and every beat of our hearts. This is the kind of healing that may finally convince us that we are loved.

Prayer: Jesus, when I am in need of a cure, give me the confidence to ask boldly and to believe it is possible. But if a cure does not come, open my heart all the wider to be healed.

Jesus Heals a Man with a Withered Hand

Mark 3:1-6

[1]Again he entered the synagogue, and a man was there who had a withered hand. [2][The Pharisees] watched him to see whether he would cure him on the sabbath, so that they might accuse him. [3]And he said to the man who had the withered hand, "Come forward." [4]Then he said to them, "Is it lawful to do good or to do harm on the sabbath, to save life or to kill?" But they were silent. [5]He looked around at them with anger; he was grieved at their hardness of heart and said to the man, "Stretch out your hand." He stretched it out, and his hand was restored. [6]The Pharisees went out and immediately conspired with the Herodians against him, how to destroy him.

11

Stretch Out Your Hand

There is so much happening in this short healing story. It is framed by mounting tension in Mark's Gospel, tension that escalates extremely early in Mark's narrative. The Pharisees are on a mission. They want to trap Jesus, ironically, through an act of his own compassion. But Jesus is also on a mission. He wants to teach them how to "save life." He wants to teach them this compassion that is the hallmark of his life.

Of course, many Pharisees of Jesus' day were compassionate men. The point is really about Jesus asking *everyone*—not just the Pharisees in the story, but every human being who has read or heard it since—to dig a little deeper, to think a little bigger, to stretch the human heart much farther. There is not one or another time that is right or wrong for caring for another human being. It is always the right time to save life, to restore health, to heal, to love. It angered and grieved Jesus that the human beings around him didn't seem to understand this. And still? We remain hard of heart, so often, in the face of others' pain.

Of course, the Pharisees in the story are not convinced by Jesus, not by his word or his deed. Rather than saving life, they plot to destroy. By the third chapter of Mark's Gospel, we know that Jesus will die.

But the heart of the story remains the healing itself. Jesus gives the man two simple instructions. The first is "Come forward." The man must step out of the shadows. Jesus wants him to be close. The second instruction is "Stretch out your hand." Echoes of Scripture may reverberate in our minds—it is always God who stretches out his hand, extending the divine reach into our world (Pss 37:24; 95:5; 138:7). Stretching, because the distance can feel so far. Stretching, because the love is so great.

Stretch out your hand, Jesus tells the man, *so I may stretch out mine and enter your world. So I may bridge the gap.*

From what we can tell, this man was not in danger of death. But Jesus considered this healing to be an act of "saving life." There is no need too small, no wound or hand or soul too insignificant, that Jesus will not call it near, call it forth, stretch to touch it, restore and save it.

Meditation: The command of Jesus to "stretch out your hand" is rich in implications for healing. By responding to Jesus, this man becomes a participant in the healing process. No longer standing by, he actively reaches toward Jesus and the healing he offers. Stretching indicates effort. Opening ourselves to healing, partnering with God, allowing ourselves to change and be changed are all difficult things to do. But to stretch is to grow. To stretch is to touch and encounter, to bridge the gap. To stretch is to be healed. Let this "spirituality of stretching" become part of your praying and living.

Prayer: Jesus, Healer, soften my heart and strengthen my will to stretch toward your compassion, so I may be changed.

A Multitude at the Seaside

Mark 3:7-10

[7]Jesus departed with his disciples to the sea, and a great multitude from Galilee followed him; [8]hearing all that he was doing, they came to him in great numbers from Judea, Jerusalem, Idumea, beyond the Jordan, and the region around Tyre and Sidon. [9]He told his disciples to have a boat ready for him because of the crowd, so that they would not crush him; [10]for he had cured many, so that all who had diseases pressed upon him to touch him.

12

Vulnerable Healer

This is a distressing scene.

Read this passage again, very slowly. Imagine the crowds growing larger and larger, following Jesus wherever he went—from town to town, across the countryside, and down to the sea. Imagine Jesus gathering his disciples around him, telling them to have a boat ready. Hear the concern, the stress, in his voice. Watch the crowds physically pressing in on him.

The needs of the world are overwhelming.

In scenes like this, Christology and reality collide to magnificent effect. Here we must again forget "the Jesus we've always known" and encounter the Jesus of the Gospels. Even if our theology tells us that Jesus *could have* healed them all with the wave of his hand or a thought of his mind, this is not who Jesus is, according to the Gospels. It is not who or how God chooses to be in the world.

God did not come into the world as a battalion of doctors armed with antibiotics, x-ray machines, and waiting rooms. God came into the world as a human being, an individual, as one man—intentionally limited, intentionally small. His compassion may have been limitless, but his body was not. There were times when Jesus had to get in a boat and drift away, because he did not want to be crushed by the overwhelming needs of the world.

Why is this magnificent, when we too have so many needs? Why is it magnificent, when there were many in the crowd that day who could not get close enough to Jesus to touch him, or to be touched?

For only one reason. As much as we are distressed by this scene, we are equally overwhelmed by the vulnerability of our savior. As much as we desire to be healed, we deeply desire a healer who understands us. And how could he understand us if he were not small? If he never feared being crushed by all that life threw at him? How could he understand if he were not really one of us?

Do not let our sophisticated Christology, our rather complicated theology that has developed over the centuries, diminish for you the raw and real Jesus we read about here in Mark 3:7-10. To be reminded that God chose limitation and vulnerability in the person of Jesus only makes his healing ministry—then and now—all the more astounding.

Meditation: As you imagine this Gospel scene, look around at the crowd with all its needs. Look at the faces of the people, one at a time. A crowd can be frightening, overwhelming. But each person there needed Jesus for some particular reason. There were children there. There were people racked with pain. There were men and women at the end of their ropes. This way of seeing the world may help us tap into the compassion of Jesus. The needs of the world really boil down to the need of the person who is nearest to you—in your own home, in your parish, in your workplace. Look with eyes that see the needs of one person at a time, and do what you can.

Prayer: Lord Jesus, your vulnerability only spurs us on to serve alongside you, to not give up on the overwhelming needs of the world.

Jesus Heals the Servant of a Roman Centurion

Matthew 8:5-10, 13

[5]When he entered Capernaum, a centurion came to him, appealing to him [6]and saying, "Lord, my servant is lying at home paralyzed, in terrible distress." [7]And he said to him, "I will come and cure him." [8]The centurion answered, "Lord, I am not worthy to have you come under my roof; but only speak the word, and my servant will be healed. [9]For I also am a man under authority, with soldiers under me; and I say to one, 'Go,' and he goes, and to another, 'Come,' and he comes, and to my slave, 'Do this,' and the slave does it." [10]When Jesus heard him, he was amazed and said to those who followed him, "Truly I tell you, in no one in Israel have I found such faith." . . . [13]And to the centurion Jesus said, "Go; let it be done for you according to your faith." And the servant was healed in that hour.

13

Pot of Gold

What a practical man, this Roman centurion! His servant is in "terrible distress," and he believes Jesus can help. Jesus offers to come, but the centurion says it isn't necessary. He understands how authority works—he believes Jesus can heal simply by authorizing it. And he is correct. His faith is admirable (Jesus himself is amazed by it), and in a sense he is quite thoughtful. He's saved Jesus the trip.

In Luke's version of this story, the centurion does not even show up! Instead he sends someone else to make the request, saying he does not "presume" to come to Jesus himself (Luke 7:7).

Practical, trusting, and humble—a fair description of the Roman centurion. But I wonder, did this practical man miss the opportunity of a lifetime?

The Gospel portrait of Jesus is clear: it was Jesus' instinct and preference to heal people by being with them. This is God's "style," as Pope Francis has described it: a style of nearness. *Could* Jesus heal from afar? Sure he could. Did he? Not very often.

When the centurion informs Jesus of his servant's illness, Jesus' immediate response is "I will come and cure him." Jesus was not concerned about practical matters like distance, or time, or whether there was an easier or more efficient way of healing. Nor was he concerned with who was "worthy" to have him enter their home. His instinct was to be in close proximity to the distressed servant: "I will come."

But the centurion is quick to say *it isn't necessary*. And apparently, it wasn't. But he has missed a golden opportunity —to have Jesus of Nazareth come under his roof. And he has missed a golden truth about healing—that it is not only about a cure but about proximity and closeness. Jesus offered not only to cure but *to be present*. This is his instinct. This is his gift.

The bottom line is always relationship. And relationships need time and presence. They need proximity. Those in relationship need to *be with one another*. The centurion got what he asked for and what he believed Jesus could give. But he could have had so much more.

As my old pastor used to say, "Why do we settle for pennies when we could have a pot of gold?"

Meditation: Do we shortchange ourselves by asking for too little? Jesus is standing by, wanting to come. Do we dismiss him too easily? Do we consider ourselves unworthy of the gold of a healing encounter?

Prayer: Jesus, when you offer to come under my roof, let me welcome you with open arms.

Jesus Heals a Man with Demons in Gerasa

Mark 5:1-20

¹They came to the other side of the sea, to the country of the Gerasenes. ²And when he had stepped out of the boat, immediately a man out of the tombs with an unclean spirit met him. ³He lived among the tombs; and no one could restrain him any more, even with a chain; ⁴for he had often been restrained with shackles and chains, but the chains he wrenched apart, and the shackles he broke in pieces; and no one had the strength to subdue him. ⁵Night and day among the tombs and on the mountains he was always howling and bruising himself with stones. ⁶When he saw Jesus from a distance, he ran and bowed down before him; ⁷and he shouted at the top of his voice, "What have you to do with me, Jesus, Son of the Most High God? I adjure you by God, do not torment me." ⁸For he had said to him, "Come out of the man, you unclean spirit!" ⁹Then Jesus asked him, "What is your name?" He replied, "My name is Legion; for we are many." ¹⁰He begged him earnestly

not to send them out of the country. [11]Now there on the hillside a great herd of swine was feeding; [12]and the unclean spirits begged him, "Send us into the swine; let us enter them." [13]So he gave them permission. And the unclean spirits came out and entered the swine; and the herd, numbering about two thousand, rushed down the steep bank into the sea, and were drowned in the sea.

[14]The swineherds ran off and told it in the city and in the country. Then people came to see what it was that had happened. [15]They came to Jesus and saw the demoniac sitting there, clothed and in his right mind, the very man who had had the legion; and they were afraid. [16]Those who had seen what had happened to the demoniac and to the swine reported it. [17]Then they began to beg Jesus to leave their neighborhood. [18]As he was getting into the boat, the man who had been possessed by demons begged him that he might be with him. [19]But Jesus refused, and said to him, "Go home to your friends, and tell them how much the Lord has done for you, and what mercy he has shown you." [20]And he went away and began to proclaim in the Decapolis how much Jesus had done for him; and everyone was amazed.

14

Legion

What is more heart-wrenching—or more terrifying—than the story of the "Gerasene demoniac," the man filled with a legion's worth of demons? Mark, always the vivid storyteller, tells us that the man lived "among the tombs" and that no one could restrain him—not with human strength, not with metal chains, not with shackles around his hands or feet. He broke them all. Not only was he strong, but he was dangerous. Mostly he seemed to take his violence out on himself, bruising himself with stones. His howling must have been terrible to hear.

Unlike those who yearn for physical healing—those who come to Jesus begging him to heal them—this man does the opposite. He also begs, *earnestly.* But he is begging Jesus to leave him alone. And yet—is it the man who is speaking, or is it Legion, the many demons? The man is so diminished that evil is having its way with him. He speaks not for himself but for demons. Even his name has been erased: "My name is Legion," he says.

A fascinating detail in this story is Jesus' response to Legion. He listens, and he accommodates. Legion does not wish to be sent out of the country but into two thousand swine. "So he gave them permission." Of course the swine, like the man, only hurt themselves.

How painful evil is. How damaging, how diminishing. As awful as the man's behavior was, the sudden death of thousands of animals is also disturbing. What is happening here?

A man who lived among the tombs, among death, whose personal strength was used only to harm himself . . . we know this man. He is *us,* living the most painful times in our lives. We too are Legion.

This doesn't mean that we are possessed, or that we are evil. But there are times of such diminishment—times of hate or pain, addiction or hopelessness, jealousy or anger—when the smell of death is all around us, and the strength of our inner thrashings breaks chains like toothpicks.

We always thought we would be the ones to seek out Jesus, to kneel in faith, begging him to heal us. But when we are Legion, we beg him to leave us alone. Alone is where we think we want to be.

Fortunately for us, Jesus wanders into Gerasa. It's Gentile territory; it isn't even where he belongs. But it is where he goes, out among the tombs. He isn't afraid of the howling, the thrashing, or the shouting. He isn't afraid when we don't even know our own names anymore, when we call ourselves by other, terrible names. It is the pain that is speaking, not us.

If this story tells us one thing, it is that Jesus is listening in such times and places. Whether it is us or the pain talking, Jesus is listening. Listening to our voices no matter what or how they speak. Listening when we do not even know who we are. Ready to shout "Go!" to what torments us uncontrollably (Matt 8:32).

The Gospel story is slow to call the man from Gerasa a "man." It continues to use the word "demoniac" even after Legion has drowned in the sea. It isn't until he begs to be with Jesus that the Gospel calls him a man again without going back to "demoniac." He is *adam*, the Hebrew word for "human"—created with love, breathed by God (Gen 2:7).

It breaks my heart when Jesus sends the man away. It may have broken Jesus' too. But he tells him, "Go home to your friends." It is a gift to the man. *Go, be surrounded by the love you deserve.*

"And tell them," he says. *Tell them what God has done, and what mercy he has shown. Tell them that God listens.*

Meditation: Some may not relate to the Gerasene demoniac, and we can all give thanks for that. Some lives have been gentler than others. But for those who see in this troubled man a kinship or a reminder of a terrible time, there is much to be explored in this great healing story. It wasn't by chance that Jesus encountered this man who lived among the tombs. He is always there when we too are Legion.

Prayer: Jesus, when pain controls me, when I beg you to leave me alone, stay with me. Send away all that harms me. And then, let me stay with you.

15

Banish the Healer

Mark's graphic story of the "Gerasene demoniac" ends with universal wonder: "everyone was amazed." But this was the response of the people of the surrounding region, those who heard about the healing. The people of the town of Gerasa, those who knew the man who called himself Legion, had a very different reaction. Mark tells us they were "afraid" and "began to beg Jesus to leave their neighborhood."

What kind of response is this to a spectacular healing? Why would people react this way after seeing a man restored to himself? This is perhaps the most incredible and almost incomprehensible part of the story. The townspeople, who were once burdened with a wild man who could not be subdued and who was so powerful that he wrenched apart chains and broke shackles into pieces, are now presented with a man "clothed and in his right mind." Why would anyone send away the person responsible for this amazing transformation?

I suppose we might ask this question all the way to the cross. There were certainly reasons people kept trying to get rid of Jesus, until they succeeded (sort of) by crucifying him. But in this case, in Gerasa, think for a moment how startling, how alarming, how supernatural and unfamiliar was this power of God on full display in the person of Jesus. Imagine standing near that cliff, hearing the demoniac unable to speak his own name, speaking only the name of demons, begging Jesus to send them into swine. Hear Jesus shout, "Go!" (Matt 8:32). Hear the thundering hoofs of the swine, and watch the dust fly until you see them do something completely unnatural for animals to do. Now see the man, utterly spent, sink to the ground.

Something happened on the cliffs of Gerasa that had people shaking. This was a power far beyond the breaking of chains and shackles. It was unfamiliar, and it frightened them. Jesus had put the finger of God directly on evil, and the drama of evil's departure was almost unbearable.

And yet there was one man who had a front-row seat but did not ask Jesus to leave. This man "begged him that he might be with him." Yes, this was the man who had been Legion, who had lived among the tombs, himself no stranger to supernatural powers. For him, there was nothing left to fear, not for his whole life.

Meditation: We understand why evil frightens us. But we may have to think a bit about why something as beautiful and sacred as saving a life can be frightening. The sacred is "other." It is set apart and special. And yet, it shouldn't feel so far out of our experience that we are frightened by it. The people of Gerasa were afraid, but the man who had been possessed by demons was not. Perhaps the experience of being broken is what opens us to the sacred as the most beautiful, the most familiar, the most tender of all realities.

Prayer: Lord Jesus, in my own brokenness, open me to the familiarity of the sacred.

Jesus Raises the Daughter of Jairus

Mark 5:21-24, 35-43

²¹When Jesus had crossed again in the boat to the other side, a great crowd gathered around him; and he was by the sea. ²²Then one of the leaders of the synagogue named Jairus came and, when he saw him, fell at his feet ²³and begged him repeatedly, "My little daughter is at the point of death. Come and lay your hands on her, so that she may be made well, and live." ²⁴So he went with him. . . . ³⁵While he was still speaking, some people came from the leader's house to say, "Your daughter is dead. Why trouble the teacher any further?" ³⁶But overhearing what they said, Jesus said to the leader of the synagogue, "Do not fear, only believe." ³⁷He allowed no one to follow him except Peter, James, and John, the brother of James. ³⁸When they came to the house of the leader of the synagogue, he saw a commotion, people weeping and wailing loudly. ³⁹When he had entered, he said to them, "Why do you make a commotion and weep? The child is not dead but sleeping." ⁴⁰And

they laughed at him. Then he put them all outside, and took the child's father and mother and those who were with him, and went in where the child was. [41]He took her by the hand and said to her, "Talitha cum," which means, "Little girl, get up!" [42]And immediately the girl got up and began to walk about (she was twelve years of age). At this they were overcome with amazement. [43]He strictly ordered them that no one should know this, and told them to give her something to eat.

16

Silence Heals

This story is full of noise. Jesus has agreed to go with Jairus, a leader of the local synagogue in Capernaum whose "little daughter is at the point of death." When he is almost to Jairus's house, the noise begins. First, people come and tell Jairus that his daughter is dead and to leave Jesus alone. Then, upon arriving at the house, Jairus and Jesus are greeted by a "commotion" of people "weeping and wailing loudly." Finally, when Jesus tells the weeping people that the little girl is not dead, they laugh.

None of these people meant any harm. Those who came to warn Jairus did not want him to be surprised to find his little girl dead; they figured it was unnecessary for Jesus to continue to the house. Those who were weeping and wailing were paying tribute to a young life lost too soon and to a family entering a time of deep grief. Even those who laughed at Jesus—they had no idea what he meant, what he could do, how serious he was.

Jesus' response to all this commotion? He threw them all out. As he entered the room where the dead child lay, he kept with him only the girl's mother and father, and a handful of his closest companions. Presumably these were people who knew how to be quiet. They understood the thin veil between life and death, how sacred it is, how fragile. They understood that Jesus wanted silence.

Mark's Gospel is known for moving quickly, but I think we might be entitled to a breath between verses 40 and 41. Yes, we might take a breath and linger for a moment, and experience the silence in that room. A silence the girl's parents may have found unbearable, devoid as it was of their daughter's chatter, or her laughter, or her breathing. A silence Jesus' disciples may have found tense as they waited to see . . . *Could he really do this?* A silence that Jesus no doubt experienced as golden. Because silence heals.

The narrative moves forward gently with Jesus taking the girl's hand, just as we would expect. He breaks the silence in words that have been preserved in Aramaic, Jesus' native tongue: *Talitha* ("Little girl"), a term of endearment, and then the command *cum* ("stand up" or "rise"). And so she lives.

Noise can be natural and good; it has its place. But sometimes we need to set it aside, send it away, enter a quiet room where silence can breathe. It's true that silence may overwhelm or even burden us at first. It may feel oppressive and only serve to exaggerate the pain or illness or evil we've come to confront or surrender. But resist the feeling—resist the temptation to allow the noise back in—until you've let yourself adjust to what has changed, until you've heard the golden sound and felt its healing rays.

Meditation: One of Scripture's greatest icons of suffering is Job, who lost everything he had, including his health. Job was determined not to blame God, but he struggled. As the book unfolds, he is plagued by questions and theories that boil down to one word: *Why?* In the end, it is not until Job chooses silence—literally saying, "I lay my hand on my mouth" (Job 40:4)—that he sees God, and hears God, and finds some measure of peace.

Prayer: Jesus, when healing is needed, lead me into silence.

Jesus Heals a Woman Who Has Suffered for Twelve Years

Mark 5:25-34

[25]Now there was a woman who had been suffering from hemorrhages for twelve years. [26]She had endured much under many physicians, and had spent all that she had; and she was no better, but rather grew worse. [27]She had heard about Jesus, and came up behind him in the crowd and touched his cloak, [28]for she said, "If I but touch his clothes, I will be made well." [29]Immediately her hemorrhage stopped; and she felt in her body that she was healed of her disease. [30]Immediately aware that power had gone forth from him, Jesus turned about in the crowd and said, "Who touched my clothes?" [31]And his disciples said to him, "You see the crowd pressing in on you; how can you say, 'Who touched me?'" [32]He looked all around to see who had done it. [33]But the woman, knowing what had happened to her, came in fear and trembling, fell down before him, and told him the whole truth. [34]He said to her, "Daughter, your faith has made you well; go in peace, and be healed of your disease."

17

Just the Fringe

Who doesn't relate to this authentic woman? She has suffered for twelve years, seen many doctors, spent everything she had. But she is no better; in fact, she is worse, the very picture of hopelessness. And yet, she has "heard about Jesus," and he is passing by.

Mark tells us once again that the crowd is pressing in on Jesus. He is surrounded, perhaps even jostled, by the crowd. Many are in need of healing. Some are just there to witness the growing phenomenon that is Jesus.

From deep within this jostling crowd, the woman steps forward. She has only one goal, one plan: to touch Jesus' clothing. Perhaps it is all she thinks she can manage with the movement of the crowd. (I imagine Jesus was one to walk at a decent clip, even when surrounded.) Or perhaps she is afraid to touch his body. Perhaps she feels unworthy or unclean. Perhaps the sight of Jesus has left her overwhelmed, intimidated. She won't touch or jostle him like the others. But neither will she give up.

Interestingly, while Mark writes that the woman "touched his cloak," Matthew and Luke both say that she touched merely the "hem" or the "fringe" of his clothing (Matt 9:20; Luke 8:44). *Just the fringe.* It is all she can manage. But it is enough. After twelve long years, healing comes in a single moment. She feels it "in her body."

Reaching for the fringe of Jesus' clothing is an image worth contemplating. When we seek healing, we may first imagine an intimate scene of encounter, like many of the Gospel stories. We imagine the hands of Jesus touching us, the eyes of Jesus focused on us, the voice of Jesus speaking to us. But this scene—with all its jostling, its rapid movement, and its arm's length interaction with the healer— might ring truer to our experience.

This woman had faith—there is no doubt about that. But she was tired—there is no doubt about that either. She believed . . . she *wanted* to believe. But she was discouraged. She had been disappointed so many times. No doubt she lived at the intersection of physical illness and inner conflict—motivated by an inner, hopeful voice, but tempered by all that life had been.

Sometimes stretching for the fringe of the healer's garment is all we can manage. It isn't a lack of faith or hope that places us there, carried along by a jostling crowd, at arm's length from Jesus. Sometimes that is just where life takes us. But the healer is there, and we've heard about him. We'll have our chance.

Elsewhere, the Gospels say that when crowds of the sick were brought to Jesus, they only asked to touch "the fringe of his cloak," and all who touched it were healed (Matt 14:36; Mark 6:56). We may long for a prolonged, intimate encounter with Jesus of Nazareth. But sometimes—no, always—just a brush with the sacred is enough to change us.

Meditation: When we are in need of healing for ourselves or a loved one, there are times when we lose hope. Sometimes bad news just keeps coming. Sometimes chronic pain wears us out. Sometimes we just can't get a handle on where life is taking us. In those times, take comfort in this story. And remember that *Jesus noticed*—the moment this woman stretched out her hand and touched his cloak, he noticed. He looked for her. And the Gospel doesn't have to say it: we know he loved her.

Prayer: Jesus, sometimes it feels as though you're just passing by, and all I can do is reach out. When that happens, please turn around and look for me. I am here.

Jesus Teaches and Heals

Luke 6:17-19

[17]He came down with them and stood on a level place, with a great crowd of his disciples and a great multitude of people from all Judea, Jerusalem, and the coast of Tyre and Sidon. [18]They had come to hear him and to be healed of their diseases; and those who were troubled with unclean spirits were cured. [19]And all in the crowd were trying to touch him, for power came out from him and healed all of them.

18

Dynamis

This sweeping passage about the teaching and healing ministry of Jesus comes right before Jesus' great sermon in Luke's Gospel, the Sermon on the Plain.

Jesus has just descended the mountain where he spent a night in prayer (Luke 6:12). He is standing now "on a level place," with and among the disciples and crowds that have gathered from as far as Tyre and Sidon, Gentile territory to the north. Luke's description here offers an interesting contrast with Matthew's account of Jesus' epic sermon (the Sermon on the Mount). In Matthew, Jesus ascends a mountain when he sees the crowds and sits down (Matt 5:1). But Luke seems to be highlighting Jesus' desire to be among the people as he describes Jesus coming down with them to a level place—literally *on their level*. And rather than assuming the classic seated position of a revered teacher as he does in Matthew, here Jesus stands. This is the stance of one who is available, mobile, and "at the ready."

We might also note the desire of the people for healing —certainly nothing new in these stories. They reach out, "trying to touch him." Luke explains that they were trying to touch Jesus because "power came out from him," a power that healed them all.

The Greek word for "power" is *dynamis*, familiar to us as the root of words like "dynamic" and "dynamite." This power is movement, life, and change. It is electric, attractive.

In Jesus' case, of course, the source of this *dynamis* is God. As both the inbreaking and outbreaking of God's kingdom on earth, Jesus is walking *dynamis*—like dynamite! And Jesus is in full possession of this power. He knows when it comes and goes from him.

Recall the story of the woman who had suffered for twelve years with a bleeding condition, who reached out from within a jostling crowd to touch the hem of Jesus' cloak (Luke 8:43-48). Jesus immediately asked, "Who touched me?" We can only imagine the look on Peter's face as he stated the obvious—that Jesus was surrounded, that the entire crowd was literally pressing in on him. But Jesus, a man of incredible awareness, replied, "I noticed that power [*dynamis*] had gone out from me" (Luke 8:46).

God's power takes many forms, but in the healing stories of Jesus, it is almost palpable. It flows out of him like a river flowing into a sea—like the river that flowed out of Eden to water the garden (Gen 2:10), like the river flowing from God's throne to nourish the tree of life, whose leaves are for the healing of the nations (Rev 22:1-2).

Meditation: Jesus' deliberate choice to stand "on a level place" with the people is directly connected to his healing power. The people reach out for him, and he is there. And so his *dynamis* flows freely to them. Once again, the presence of Jesus is the key to healing. God's power is not something that is "out there," beyond us. It is within and among us.

Prayer: Lord Jesus, you freely share your power with us, power that flows from your deep well of compassion. May we too stand on level ground with those who need us, and may your love flow from us like a river.

Jesus Heals Many at Peter's House

Matthew 8:16-17

[16]That evening they brought to him many who were possessed with demons; and he cast out the spirits with a word, and cured all who were sick. [17]This was to fulfill what had been spoken through the prophet Isaiah, "He took our infirmities and bore our diseases."

19

The Closing of Day

Like Luke's account of Jesus healing at sunset, Matthew describes Jesus healing in the evening. It is exhausting to think of Jesus healing so many people at the end of a long day. Did he ever stop working? At the same time, these scenes bring us peace. The closing of the day is a healing time. It is often when we need him most.

Along with the brief description of the evening scene and a rather remarkable reference to Jesus' power over evil (casting out spirits with only "a word"), Matthew links a verse from the prophet Isaiah (53:4) with Jesus' healing ministry. In the time of Isaiah's ministry, the verse likely referred to Israel, the faithful, suffering servant of God. Here, the verse suggests that Jesus himself, in some way, has *taken on* the pain of the people. Apparently, illnesses and infirmities do not simply disappear into thin air.

Of course, just as every healing foreshadows the resurrection of Jesus, every infirmity foreshadows his death. The infirmities he takes on as a healer are not unlike those he bears as the savior of the world. Every evil that besets us is his business, his work. Every pain will be healed but first must be taken on, assumed by the one who has become like us so that we might become like him.

Every parent wishes they could do this—take on their child's pain. A loving friend wants nothing more than to shoulder the other's burden. We want to do these things, but we can't, not completely. Jesus can. The *how* remains a mystery, though we know it is accomplished by love.

In the quiet of evening, our burdens can feel the heaviest. Let's allow Jesus to do his work. He is not too tired or too burdened already. In the evening, he cured them all.

Meditation: Reflect on a time when you've instinctively wanted to take on someone else's pain or burden. How would you describe that feeling? Did you find some way to share that burden, even if you couldn't take it away completely? Now reflect on Jesus feeling the same, and doing the same, for you.

Prayer: Jesus, Healer and Savior, thank you for taking our pain and bearing our burdens.

Jesus Heals Two Men Who Are Blind

Matthew 9:27-30

[27]As Jesus went on from there, two blind men followed him, crying loudly, "Have mercy on us, Son of David!" [28]When he entered the house, the blind men came to him; and Jesus said to them, "Do you believe that I am able to do this?" They said to him, "Yes, Lord." [29]Then he touched their eyes and said, "According to your faith let it be done to you." [30]And their eyes were opened.

20

When the Cure Doesn't Come

Like the story of the man with a skin disease in Mark 1:40-42, this story of the healing of two men who are blind is quite straightforward. Addressing Jesus with two titles ("Son of David" and "Lord"), the men ask Jesus for mercy—they want to see again. Jesus asks if they believe, and they say, "Yes." And Jesus responds as we expect. He touches their eyes, and their eyes are opened: "According to your faith let it be done to you."

It seems so simple. *According to your faith let it be done to you.* But did Matthew know, when he put pen to parchment, that these words could someday mystify, even sting? Because not all who are blind, even those with great faith, will see again.

Reflection on Jesus' healing ministry must at last confront this painful truth. Some sick people won't get better. Some dead people will stay dead. Some who come, who ask—who *beg*—will not receive what they ask for, no matter how deeply they believe.

And here is where we must return again and again, in any matter of faith and prayer: Jesus the Healer is no less with us now than then. The time for miracles has not come to an end. It is not time to stop asking, to stop looking Jesus in the eye or kneeling before him in total vulnerability or reaching for the hem of his garment. It is not time to stop whispering his name or saying with these men of Matthew's Gospel, "Have mercy!"

And we must believe that all of our asking and whispering—whether for ourselves or someone we love, whether offered in a state of great faith or faith that's just hanging by a thread—is heard.

But we know God does not answer every prayer in the way we hope. Sometimes our bodies continue to bear tremendous burdens. Sometimes pain is—and remains—part of us. Sometimes illness is—and remains—part of us. Sometimes disability is—and remains—part of us. To live this imperfection is not to say that we are loved less by God, or that God is not paying attention. But it is to say that imperfection is the human experience, for now. And it will be until we experience *salvation,* not a cure.

There is a difference between curing and healing. Jesus has cured many, but he will heal us all. Dramatic cures, restoration of sight and hearing, the defeat of paralysis—these are very real signs of the inbreaking of God's kingdom. But *healing*—of minds, hearts, relationships, communities—is the final, the enduring, sign that God is with us.

Meditation: We have all known times when a cure did not come. When this happens, we don't know or understand why. But we do know that the promise of God to neither leave us nor forsake us stands firm (Deut 31:8; Heb 13:5). The presence of God is our salvation. It is our healing. It is forever.

Prayer: Jesus, Healer, I trust in your care for me and those I love. When I ask for a cure, I believe you can do it. But above all else, and no matter what happens, I trust that you are always reaching out to me with a healing hand.

Jesus' Compassion for the Crowds

Matthew 9:35-36

[35]Then Jesus went about all the cities and villages, teaching in their synagogues, and proclaiming the good news of the kingdom, and curing every disease and every sickness. [36]When he saw the crowds, he had compassion for them, because they were harassed and helpless, like sheep without a shepherd.

21

Reservoir

When he saw the crowds, he had compassion for them.
This statement may not seem particularly remarkable, given
the stories we've been reading. We know Jesus is compassionate. Compassion is the energizing force behind his
healing ministry.

But what is remarkable about this summary statement
that describes Jesus going about "all the cities and villages,"
teaching and healing and still finding within himself a deep
well of compassion, is the fact that it comes at the end of
an almost stupefying number of healings, all told in the
single breath of Matthew 8–9: a man with a skin disease,
the centurion's servant, Peter's mother-in-law, two men
with demons, a man who was paralyzed, the synagogue
official's daughter, a woman with a hemorrhage, two men
who were blind, and a man who had a spirit that prevented
him from speaking.

Of course, we know that Jesus healed entire crowds in
the span of a single evening. But the effect of Matthew's

highly concentrated catalog of healings comes down to this: Jesus' mission to live and proclaim the kingdom of God is on fire.

It is indeed remarkable that, at the end of this healing litany, Jesus looks around at the people who continue to surround him and simply feels compassion. He doesn't see endless, draining need. He doesn't see selfishness or darkness or other things that can make humans so unlovable (or at least unlikable). No, Jesus sees people like a shepherd sees sheep: they are his responsibility. Over every hill, and around every bend, there are always more sheep, and it's rare to find one that isn't at least a bit on the hapless side.

So any time we wonder if Jesus might be getting tired of corralling us, feeding us, or healing us, we've only to look back at Matthew 8–9. Though it may exhaust *us* to read it, the Gospel is clear that Jesus' own reservoir of compassion, awareness, and tenderness is quite undiminished. His mission, like the Healer himself, is unstoppable.

Meditation: Immediately after these verses, Jesus looks to his disciples and says, "The harvest is plentiful, but the laborers are few" (Matt 9:37). Jesus sees the field of human need as yielding a rich harvest, but the field itself must be tended. What might be harvested from your own need for healing and wholeness? What is the fruit of your struggle? And how might you be called to labor in this field, to serve the needs of others?

Prayer: Jesus, Good Shepherd of all who feel helpless and harassed, remind us of your endless compassion. Around every bend and over every hill, may we find you searching for us without fail, extending a hand to guide and to heal.

Jesus Raises a Mother's Son in Nain

Luke 7:11-15

[11]Soon afterwards he went to a town called Nain, and his disciples and a large crowd went with him. [12]As he approached the gate of the town, a man who had died was being carried out. He was his mother's only son, and she was a widow; and with her was a large crowd from the town. [13]When the Lord saw her, he had compassion for her and said to her, "Do not weep." [14]Then he came forward and touched the bier, and the bearers stood still. And he said, "Young man, I say to you, rise!" [15]The dead man sat up and began to speak, and Jesus gave him to his mother.

22

Her Only Son

Surely the man from Nain was not the first dead person Jesus had ever seen. Death and funerals were common. And yet there are very few stories of Jesus raising the dead in the Gospels. Very few. Perhaps he considered death as sacred as life. It wasn't something to be disrupted.

And yet, on occasion, it is almost as though Jesus' compassion gets the better of him: Jairus falling at his feet, begging for the life of his daughter (Mark 5:22-23); Mary of Bethany, shattered because Jesus has arrived too late to save her brother (John 11:32-33); and this woman, already a widow, following the funeral bier of her only son. We know she is weeping, because we hear Jesus telling her to stop. We know she is weeping, because Jesus' compassion is ignited within him. It is *people* that move Jesus—people loving people.

The touch of Jesus is curious. Typically he touches the person in need of healing. Here he touches only the bier, the frame on which the coffin rests, the frame for carrying death. It is all that is needed. He commands the young man to rise, and then he "[gives] him to his mother." We might hear an echo here of Jesus giving another young man, his Beloved Disciple, to his own mother, at another time when death and life hang in the air.

This story reminds us that every physical healing is also a social one. Healing is a profound transformation for the one who is healed, but it is also the restoration of those who love them. We can only imagine the heartbreak of this mother, a pain that Jesus could not bear, and the restoration of that heart as her son "began to speak." Surely the first word of his new life was "Mother."

Meditation: The healing of relationships is as miraculous as any physical healing. People are restored to each other in many beautiful ways—through physical healing that allows a relationship to continue, through the miracle of forgiveness, by clearing up misunderstandings, by giving one another the benefit of the doubt, living the Golden Rule, loving our enemies, and recognizing Christ alive and vibrant in one another. Every relationship can be healed, even if it takes a miracle. Ask Jesus for that miracle. And be open to every opportunity to extend his compassion to all that is broken, even to what appears to be dead, in this world.

Prayer: Jesus, is there anything you can't do? In restoring this man to his mother, you remind us that even death can be overcome—physically, spiritually, and communally. Touch what is dead in us so we too may rise.

Jesus Heals a Man at the Pool of Bethesda

John 5:2-9

²Now in Jerusalem by the Sheep Gate there is a pool, called in Hebrew Beth-zatha, which has five porticoes. ³In these lay many invalids—blind, lame, and paralyzed. ⁵One man was there who had been ill for thirty-eight years. ⁶When Jesus saw him lying there and knew that he had been there a long time, he said to him, "Do you want to be made well?" ⁷The sick man answered him, "Sir, I have no one to put me into the pool when the water is stirred up; and while I am making my way, someone else steps down ahead of me." ⁸Jesus said to him, "Stand up, take your mat and walk." ⁹At once the man was made well, and he took up his mat and began to walk.

23

No One

The man featured in this story has been ill (paralyzed or so ill he cannot walk) for thirty-eight years. He has carried a tremendous burden. But there is another tragedy here: no one seems to care.

Jesus encounters this man in Jerusalem, near the Sheep Gate at the north end of the city, at the pool of Bethesda (or "Beth-zatha"). This pool or reservoir was believed to have healing powers when its waters were moving, which explains why so many who desired healing were there.

According to John's account, upon seeing the man, Jesus knows he has been there for a long time. The man has come so close to the pool and its healing waters, but as he explains to Jesus, there is "no one" to put him into the pool while the waters are moving. By the time he gets there (by dragging himself?), it is too late.

As contemporary readers, it is unclear to us what was really going on in this pool of Bethesda. We aren't told what Jesus thought about the pool, or if those who gathered there were really being healed by it. But there is one thing I believe we do know—and that is why Jesus singles this man out, why he goes directly to him (unusual but not unheard of in a healing story) and asks him if wants to be made well. This man's life is devoid of compassion. A simple act of human kindness could conceivably change his life forever, but there is no one to extend it. "I have no one," the man says. Jesus simply won't stand for it.

Here we might recall the man whose friends went to such lengths to lower him through the roof of the house where Jesus was staying (Mark 2:4). Even if that man had never been physically healed, he had the grace of compassionate people in his life. He was loved. This man? He has no such thing. Forget about being carried for miles, lowered through a hole in a roof, and delivered straight to Jesus—this man has no one to move him ten feet into a pool of water!

We are comforted by the healing Jesus provides for this man who has been ill for so long, but our consciences are still pricked by the story, and rightly so. We all have the power to heal—not in the same way that Jesus heals, but with the same compassion—if we so choose.

Where are the healing waters and the people who are so close to them but cannot get there without our help? Who can we carry just a small distance, entirely for their own sake? They may be heavy; it will cost us. But a person who has no one? We simply can't stand for it.

Meditation: *I have no one to put me into the pool.* The healing ministry of Jesus continues in us, whether we are called to serve as loving friends, devoted caregivers, or compassionate strangers. The sacrifice is often one of time or of "digging deep" into an inner well of patience or compassion. When we discover that well within us, we may be surprised to find it is full of healing waters.

Prayer: Jesus, your power emerged from your compassion. Help us to draw water from our own deep wells of compassion, so we too may offer the healing power of tender, quiet, steady care to those who need it most.

Jesus Heals the Sick in Gennesaret

Mark 6:53-56

[53]When they had crossed over, they came to land at Gennesaret and moored the boat. [54]When they got out of the boat, people at once recognized him, [55]and rushed about that whole region and began to bring the sick on mats to wherever they heard he was. [56]And wherever he went, into villages or cities or farms, they laid the sick in the marketplaces, and begged him that they might touch even the fringe of his cloak; and all who touched it were healed.

24

God with Us

Mark's four verses about Jesus healing at Gennesaret begin with frenetic activity. Jesus and his disciples have crossed over the Sea of Galilee. After they arrive and moor the boat (a nice Markan detail), Jesus is immediately recognized by the people of Gennesaret. His reputation has obviously preceded him. The people "rush about" the entire region, bringing the sick on mats. Wherever Jesus goes—villages, cities, farms, marketplaces—they bring their sick, and all who touch "even the fringe of his cloak" are healed. There is something about being *that close* to Jesus.

Later, after the ascension of Jesus, it will be said that Peter's shadow, when it falls on the sick, heals them (Acts 5:15). Handkerchiefs and aprons touched to the body of Paul and then touched to the bodies of the sick heal them, too (Acts 19:12). This is not about magic but about proximity, *sacred* proximity. It is how Jesus healed and continues to heal.

The human desire for healing is strong—so strong that we bring ourselves and our sick in every hope of stepping into that proximity, that sacred space. Sometimes we aren't sure whether God is totally other, totally *beyond*, or as close to us as the air we breathe and the world we can reach out and touch. The Gospels witness dramatically to both realities—God is other *and* God is with us.

And so we bring it all—illness, stress, grief, regret, resentment, anger, hate, dying, death—into that sacred space of God-with-us. And when we do, we'll know he is drawing near to us, too—mooring his boat at the water's edge, walking through every part of our lives—village, city, farm, marketplace—work, home, body, soul—drawing so close that we can hear the rustle of his cloak, its soft hem brushing the earth.

Meditation: Jesus continues to heal wherever love and compassion cast their gentle shadows across the earth. Where have you felt that sacred presence? Who has moored their boat close to the edge of your emotional, spiritual, or physical struggle? When have you heard the rustle of Jesus' cloak or felt the softness of its hem between your fingers?

Prayer: Jesus, draw near. Be as close to me as the air I breathe.

Jesus Heals the Daughter
of a Syrophoenician Woman

Mark 7:24-30

24From there he set out and went away to the region of Tyre. He entered a house and did not want anyone to know he was there. Yet he could not escape notice, 25but a woman whose little daughter had an unclean spirit immediately heard about him, and she came and bowed down at his feet. 26Now the woman was a Gentile, of Syrophoenician origin. She begged him to cast the demon out of her daughter. 27He said to her, "Let the children be fed first, for it is not fair to take the children's food and throw it to the dogs." 28But she answered him, "Sir, even the dogs under the table eat the children's crumbs." 29Then he said to her, "For saying that, you may go—the demon has left your daughter." 30So she went home, found the child lying on the bed, and the demon gone.

25

Tired

As deep as Jesus' compassion was, as bottomless as his reservoir seemed to be, as much as his *dynamis* overflowed, there were times when he was simply tired.

He entered a house and did not want anyone to know he was there. These words are as shocking as anything else in this story. We know that Jesus was human, and human beings get tired. But we almost expect the Gospels to hide it—whether to protect Jesus or to protect us, I am not sure. And, indeed, it is only in Mark's Gospel that we read this detail (Matthew tells the story but doesn't include this sentence; 15:21-28).

I suppose there could be other explanations for why Jesus didn't want anyone to know where he was. But I prefer this simple, honest, human one: he was tired. On this night, as the sun was setting, he didn't want to be needed. Like an exhausted parent at the end of a long day: "I only want a moment's peace."

But Mark's next sentence tells the fuller story: "Yet he could not escape notice." He had healed so many—

multitudes! His reputation preceded him; a "moment's peace" was unlikely to ever be his again.

The encounter and the conversation that follows are certainly unusual. Jesus initially rebuffs the woman's request, but as we would expect of any parent of a seriously ill child, she is not so easily put off. After all, she has nothing to lose and everything to gain.

Is this conversation between Jesus and the Syrophoenician woman a debate about whether Jesus' healing ministry is for Jews or Gentiles? Perhaps. If so, the conclusion of that debate seems pretty clear: God's special love for Israel is expansive and inclusive; it does not exclude others. But the undercurrent of this scene may be less about race or religion and more about shared humanity. Jesus is tired. He wants nothing more than to be alone this night, but he is needed by a mother who loves her child.

And so, just like an exhausted parent at the end of a long day, he plunges ever deeper into his inner reservoir, to see the woman before him—to really see and hear her—even to love her, even to admire her, even to heal both mother and child.

Meditation: It can be mind-bending to imagine Jesus utterly exhausted and needing to be alone. We know his compassion was without limit—but his human body was not. Jesus entering into our humanity means that he shared in our limits, experienced our exhaustion, and had to dig deep at times like this to serve others. At first, this may seem to weaken our image of Jesus. But in reality, it shows incredible strength. Even with limits, even when exhausted, he still chose to serve. He still chose to heal. He still chose to love.

Prayer: Lord Jesus, even when I am exhausted and depleted, help me to dig deep and find the strength—your strength—to love.

Jesus Heals a Man Who Is Deaf

Mark 7:31-37

[31]Then he returned from the region of Tyre, and went by way of Sidon towards the Sea of Galilee, in the region of the Decapolis. [32]They brought to him a deaf man who had an impediment in his speech; and they begged him to lay his hand on him. [33]He took him aside in private, away from the crowd, and put his fingers into his ears, and he spat and touched his tongue. [34]Then looking up to heaven, he sighed and said to him, "Ephphatha," that is, "Be opened." [35]And immediately his ears were opened, his tongue was released, and he spoke plainly. [36]Then Jesus ordered them to tell no one; but the more he ordered them, the more zealously they proclaimed it. [37]They were astounded beyond measure, saying, "He has done everything well; he even makes the deaf to hear and the mute to speak."

26

Be Opened

As Jesus travels through the Decapolis, a Gentile region of ten cities east of the Jordan, the people of the area bring him a man who cannot hear or speak, begging Jesus to "lay his hand on him." As it turns out, they get a lot more than the laying on of Jesus' hand—they get his fingers in the man's ears and mouth, plus spitting!

What a beautiful story of human accompaniment. We know Jesus can heal simply by speaking, and that he can even heal from afar. But we also know this is not his preference. He prefers to be with people, in close proximity.

It's significant that before healing the man, Jesus takes him "away from the crowd." We can't be sure why Jesus does this, but we can speculate. Does Jesus sense that the crowds are excited to see a wonder-worker but don't really care about *healing*? Does he sense that the man is uncomfortable with spectators, a private soul who quakes at the thought of being surrounded by a gazing crowd? Or does Jesus know that this healing will require particular attention—total focus—both for the sake of the physical cure and, even more critically, for the healing of the man?

All three may be true, a reflection of Jesus' remarkable intuition. And in this case, although I believe Jesus cared about the crowds and looked on them with love, he instinctively knows this is a time to focus on a single human being. So he takes the man "aside in private, away from the crowd." We can imagine the man's relief. And in the quiet, away from the noise, we can imagine Jesus' uninterrupted focus on this man and *all* his needs—seeing before him not only "a deaf man who had an impediment in his speech" but a man whose life has been full of both deep joys and deep sorrows, whose future feels uncertain, and who—like all of us—yearns for the healing presence of God in every crack and crevice of his life.

Some healing stories are so simple. Jesus touches or speaks, and the healing occurs. But some are more involved and even get a bit messy. This is one of the messy variety. The healing requires several steps (fingers in the man's ears, spitting, touching the man's tongue, speaking a command), and we get the sense that real effort is needed (moving away from the crowd for focus, looking up to heaven, sighing). Again, we can only speculate as to why this healing is more involved than most others. Perhaps it is the physical cure that requires so much effort on Jesus' part. Or perhaps the physical aspect of the cure is simply one piece of a healing that is so profound—the healing of an entire life, perhaps—that Jesus has to focus and pray and speak and touch and *sigh* in order to achieve it.

At the end of the story, the man can hear and speak. His ears are opened, his tongue released. These are physical outcomes, the results of a cure. But we know there is even more happening here. This man has been accompanied. Walking with him away from the crowds, the healer from Nazareth touched *every part* of his life, not only his ears and his tongue.

Ephphatha: Be opened! Presence heals.

Meditation: The drama of this healing story can distract us from its very essence, which is the healing power of encounter and accompaniment. Imagine yourself in this Gospel scene. You have been brought into the presence of Jesus, and he chooses to take you away from the crowd, to focus on you and every crack and crevice of your life—your past, your present, your future. What does "away from the crowd" look like for you? Look around at the scene and at your healer, who is focused on you completely. What does Jesus do or say? What healing will this encounter bring about?

Prayer: Jesus, you heal us by being with us. Teach us by your example to encounter and accompany, to be a focused, healing presence.

Jesus Heals a Woman Who Is Bent Over

Luke 13:10-13

[10]Now he was teaching in one of the synagogues on the sabbath. [11]And just then there appeared a woman with a spirit that had crippled her for eighteen years. She was bent over and was quite unable to stand up straight. [12]When Jesus saw her, he called her over and said, "Woman, you are set free from your ailment." [13]When he laid his hands on her, immediately she stood up straight and began praising God.

27

Bent Over

This story, found only in Luke's Gospel, is another healing story where Jesus takes the initiative. He sees a woman who can't stand up straight, calls her over, and immediately heals her.

We know very little about this woman—the entire story is just a handful of sentences. She has no name. She has no dialogue. One terse phrase seems to define her: she is "bent over." Can you imagine this woman, this life? For eighteen years, looking down at the ground. For eighteen years, struggling to see faces, sky, stars.

How might we relate to this unnamed woman who was noticed by Jesus? How can we enter into her experience and share in her joyful praise?

We might start by recognizing that her physical ailment is our spiritual one. We're all bent. We know just what it means to be stuck in one position, staring at the ground, to be hurting for a long time. To be unable to look someone in the eye or behold the open sky or see the stars. To yearn for nothing more than to stand up straight, to rid ourselves of some crippling spirit.

Of course, as soon as we realize we're as bent over as this woman, it's only logical to believe that Jesus notices us, too. He'll be calling us and reaching out his hands—if we're listening, if we'll come.

The woman's response to healing is both physical and spiritual. She "[stands] up straight" and praises God. Her body responds to the healing touch of Jesus' hands. What was bent over is now straightened—it must have felt wonderful! So wonderful, in fact, that the woman breaks out in praise—I imagine loud singing of a psalm of her own making: "Great is the Lord, and greatly to be praised! He has healed my infirmity, he has set me free, he has straightened my life with his outstretched hand!" And she sang, no doubt, while looking at his face, hands raised to the glory of the open sky, hoping for clear weather and the setting of the sun so she could behold the stars for the first time in many years.

What psalm will we sing, when we stand up straight? What face, what stars, will we behold?

Meditation: The woman in this story is both cured and healed. Many of us need a cure, but we *all* need healing. What inner illness have you carried for a long time? How has it "bent" your life? In what way do you feel stuck? What is this burden preventing you from seeing or doing? If you cannot raise your head, just listen. Listen for the sound of Jesus' voice.

Prayer: Compassionate Healer, you seek us out even when we are not seeking you. Call out to us when we don't see you. Stretch out your hands to heal and straighten us, that we may see your face.

Jesus Cures Many on the Mountain

Matthew 15:29-31

[29]After Jesus had left that place, he passed along the Sea of Galilee, and he went up the mountain, where he sat down. [30]Great crowds came to him, bringing with them the lame, the maimed, the blind, the mute, and many others. They put them at his feet, and he cured them, [31]so that the crowd was amazed when they saw the mute speaking, the maimed whole, the lame walking, and the blind seeing. And they praised the God of Israel.

28

Great Crowds

Lest we forget it, Matthew's scene of Jesus healing along the Sea of Galilee reminds us: Jesus was a phenomenon. Not in the sense of a celebrity or spectacle, but in the sense of having total command over all that ails us. Every phrase of this brief description of Jesus' healing ministry speaks of his authority.

He went up the mountain. Biblically speaking, the mountaintop is a place of human-divine encounter. Is it Jesus who is encountering God on the mountain? Or is it the people? It is both, of course.

He sat down. The sitting position is the stance of the great teacher, the authority figure. While the Gospels often depict Jesus as standing or walking, here he is specifically described as sitting down. And while he is typically the one on the move, going out to the people, here he is receiving them.

Great crowds came to him. It is not unusual to see crowds around Jesus, but Matthew's description of "great crowds" only builds the image of Jesus the Healer, seated on a mountain, receiving every human need.

Bringing the lame, the maimed, the blind, the mute, and many others. Never has "and many others" been so full of possibility for a healing scene, or for us. "Great crowds" must include every kind of person and every kind of need, every human desire for healing and wholeness. Certainly, some seek a physical cure, others restoration of another kind.

They put them at his feet, and he cured them. The image of people and burdens being placed at the feet of Jesus is a powerful one. Some surely come of their own volition; some are brought by others. This too should be our way: to lay it all at his feet for curing and healing, to rest in confidence that he is masterful and capable, to bring others and ourselves. At the feet of the teacher is also where disciples sit; it is the place where we learn. What will we learn, here on this mountain? What you learn might be different from what I learn. It will depend on the healing we seek.

The crowd was amazed. It is not unusual that signs and wonders amaze the people and amaze us. As they say of Jesus elsewhere, "He has done everything well" (Mark 7:37).

And they praised the God of Israel. Amazement leading to praise is a sign of both authentic healing and authentic witness to healing. Those who are healed and those who have brought them marvel and give thanks. They spontaneously understand that the glory is God's alone.

We are not told how long Jesus sat on that mountain, healing "great crowds" of human need. Was it from sunrise to sunset? Or was it even longer—his authority and power, like the very heart of God, reigning from sunrise to sunrise, embracing every soul and moment in between?

Meditation: Choose a phrase from this description of Jesus' healing ministry that resonates with you right now. Reflect on why it is meaningful to you and what God may be saying to you in this phrase. Spend several minutes slowly repeating the phrase and imagining this great healing scene on the mountain.

Prayer: Jesus, from sunrise to sunrise, we place ourselves and one another at your feet. May we join together in grateful praise.

Jesus Heals a Man Who Is Blind at Bethsaida

Mark 8:22-25

[22]They came to Bethsaida. Some people brought a blind man to him and begged him to touch him. [23]He took the blind man by the hand and led him out of the village; and when he had put saliva on his eyes and laid his hands on him, he asked him, "Can you see anything?" [24]And the man looked up and said, "I can see people, but they look like trees, walking." [25]Then Jesus laid his hands on his eyes again; and he looked intently and his sight was restored, and he saw everything clearly.

29

Presence and Process

This is a story about eyes and sight. But it is also about hands and touch.

The word "hand" is mentioned three times in just four verses. The first is a mention of the man's hand—which is presumably held by Jesus' hand as the two of them walk out of the village together, away from the man's fellow villagers, out to a quiet place. I imagine Jesus holding the man's hand quite firmly. After all, the man couldn't see the look in Jesus' eyes. But perhaps he could feel in his hand Jesus saying to him, *I will heal you.*

This story is about eyes and hands—but also saliva! The Gospels are vivid. After applying his own saliva to the man's eyes, Jesus "laid his hands" on him, twice. The first time, the healing seems partial. The man can see people (the villagers have apparently followed them), but they look like "trees, walking." That's not what people should look like! So Jesus lays his hands on the man's eyes again. This time he sees everything clearly. Healing is not always—healing is not usually—instantaneous.

The sensations of Jesus' touch must have been particularly powerful for this man, as focused as he must have been on Jesus' presence, as much as he must have perceived Jesus as a lifeline, a savior. No doubt the same gentle pressure with which Jesus held his hand Jesus now applied to his eyes. All of this holding and pressing and presence—it is an astonishingly intimate scene of effort and love.

Haven't we walked that road with Jesus out to a quiet place, felt the grip of his hand when we couldn't see the light in his eyes, felt his hands on our eyes and faces? I pray we have. I imagine us under a fig tree, just off the main road, outside of the village. Patient, focused, palpably present—healing us slowly and with love—until we too see everything clearly.

Meditation: Although many healings in the Gospels happen in an instant, this story may be a bit more relatable for most of us. Healing, whether physical or spiritual, is usually a process. Things may be "fuzzy" for a while, out of focus, not feeling right. We may get better and then get worse again. But hold on to the intimacy and the process of this healing story. Jesus will stay with you on this road just outside of the village, for as long as it takes.

Prayer: Jesus, accompany us along the way. Help us walk with patience when the road feels long. May the firm grip of your hand give us hope that you will heal us.

Jesus Heals a Boy with a Spirit

Mark 9:14-29

[14]When they came to the disciples, they saw a great crowd around them, and some scribes arguing with them. [15]When the whole crowd saw [Jesus], they were immediately overcome with awe, and they ran forward to greet him. [16]He asked them, "What are you arguing about with them?" [17]Someone from the crowd answered him, "Teacher, I brought you my son; he has a spirit that makes him unable to speak; [18]and whenever it seizes him, it dashes him down; and he foams and grinds his teeth and becomes rigid; and I asked your disciples to cast it out, but they could not do so." [19]He answered them, "You faithless generation, how much longer must I be among you? How much longer must I put up with you? Bring him to me." [20]And they brought the boy to him. When the spirit saw him, immediately it convulsed the boy, and he fell on the ground and rolled about, foaming at the mouth. [21]Jesus asked the father, "How long has this been happening

to him?" And he said, "From childhood. [22]It has often cast him into the fire and into the water, to destroy him; but if you are able to do anything, have pity on us and help us." [23]Jesus said to him, "If you are able!—All things can be done for the one who believes." [24]Immediately the father of the child cried out, "I believe; help my unbelief!" [25]When Jesus saw that a crowd came running together, he rebuked the unclean spirit, saying to it, "You spirit that keeps this boy from speaking and hearing, I command you, come out of him, and never enter him again!" [26]After crying out and convulsing him terribly, it came out, and the boy was like a corpse, so that most of them said, "He is dead." [27]But Jesus took him by the hand and lifted him up, and he was able to stand. [28]When he had entered the house, his disciples asked him privately, "Why could we not cast it out?" [29]He said to them, "This kind can come out only through prayer."

30

In Gritty, Gospel Detail

You have to hand it to Mark—he knew how to tell a healing story.

The story of the boy with "a spirit" has parallels in Matthew (17:14-21) and Luke (9:37-43). But neither of those accounts holds a candle to this one. The graphic details that Mark alone provides—from the foaming at the mouth and convulsing to the intense discussion between Jesus and the boy's father—not only give us the feeling that we are there, but they give us the sense that we can see everything in perfect focus and hear everything in intimate detail—every shout, every whisper, every breath.

I've always wondered why Mark sometimes slowed down to tell a story like this. As fast-paced as his narrative and his Messiah are, one might think he would cruise right through this sort of story, telling a more bare-bones version. But Mark was sharing Gospel—*good news*. I suppose he knew that for us to understand that news, we needed to experience it. I sure get that feeling when I read this story.

You wouldn't know it from the excerpt we have here, but immediately before this story is the account of the transfiguration of Jesus. Jesus has just descended from the mountain, where his face shone and his clothes dazzled, where he conversed with the ancients Elijah and Moses. But Jesus has not gotten too caught up in the glory of that experience. He's clearly ready to get back to work. He immediately engages with the disciples, the crowd, and the boy's father.

The father describes his son's terrible situation. Because of "a spirit," the boy is unable to speak—a painful reality, for sure. But perhaps even more startling is the violent way the spirit throws him to the ground—or into water, or into a fire. This spirit seems bent on the boy's misery and destruction. "Bring him to me," says Jesus.

As soon as Jesus says these words, we know a showdown is coming. And in Markan fashion, it happens quickly. Jesus sees a crowd "running together"—so he acts immediately, before more harm can come to the boy or anyone else: "You spirit that keeps this boy from speaking and hearing, I command you, come out of him, and never enter him again!" Jesus shouts. The spirit shouts back—crying out and convulsing the boy one last brutal time, then abruptly departing. The boy is left rigid, "like a corpse." But Jesus takes him by the hand and "lift[s] him up" (*egeiren*).

Read the story again when you have time to contemplate it—take in all of its beautiful, violent detail. It is the details that make us realize what has happened here—something miraculous, yes, but also something intensely loving: a father's love for his son, a healer's love for them both, and all of it leading to *egeiro*—rising.

Meditation: The Gospel narratives sometimes speak of "spirits" and "demons" where, in a contemporary setting, we might speak of physical disabilities, illnesses such as epilepsy, or mental health conditions. This is not to discount the language or authenticity of Scripture but to be clear that our struggles are not so different. No matter what drama a Gospel story holds, and no matter how much its details may differ from our own experiences, its central truths—the reality of human suffering; the resilience of faith; and the love, compassion, and power of Jesus—remain.

Prayer: Jesus, the glory of your transfiguration led you right back into the gritty reality of human experience. Comfort us with the knowledge that when we suffer, you are truly right beside us.

31

A Parent's Prayer

The conversation between Jesus and the father of the boy who could not speak breaks the heart of every parent. And gives us hope.

Compared to the rapid pace of the narrative surrounding it, I can't reiterate enough how dramatically time slows down in this story. As in the story of the "Gerasene demoniac," here Mark very deliberately slows his pace to share vivid details—details that Matthew and Luke do not include. One of those details is the extended dialogue between Jesus and the boy's father. Finally, we are experiencing something in "real time" rather than in fast-paced Markan time.

Here is their direct dialogue, without any narrative:

> "Teacher, I brought you my son; he has a spirit that makes him unable to speak; and whenever it seizes him, it dashes him down; and he foams and grinds his teeth and becomes rigid; and I asked your disciples to cast it out, but they could not do so."

"How long has this been happening to him?"

"From childhood. It has often cast him into the fire and into the water, to destroy him; but if you are able to do anything, have pity on us and help us."

"If you are able!—All things can be done for the one who believes."

"I believe; help my unbelief!"

Every parent or grandparent can relate to this scene. Beginning with the words "I brought you my son," we know by heart every word this father says—every word of it a prayer. *Lord, I bring you my child.*

We can imagine this man, who has very intentionally brought his son to Jesus, suddenly looking Jesus in the eye and realizing what is happening. He may feel rushed or nervous or under pressure—or perhaps he too realizes that time has slowed down. Jesus, so often on the move, is raptly attentive. He sees the boy convulsing before him. He is concerned.

"How long has this been happening?" Jesus asks, like a doctor gathering information before making a diagnosis.

The man describes the length and nature of the struggle and then, humbly, says: "If you are able to do anything, have pity on us and help us." *Lord, my child has been struggling for a long time. Please, help us.*

Of course, Jesus takes great exception to the father's use of the word "if," but this is really more of a lesson for us—a lesson for the ages—than for this man. The father couldn't possibly be more authentic. He responds as best he can: "I believe; help my unbelief!" Not only the prayer of a parent, this is the archetypal prayer of every believing person.

The father's faith—whether strong or in shreds—and the healer's power result in the boy's full recovery. The only dialogue that remains is the utterance of the crowd—"He is dead" (entirely erroneous and a much greater offense than the father's "if")—and the exchange between Jesus and his stupefied disciples:

"Why could we not cast it out?"
   "This kind can come out only through prayer."

We always thought Jesus was talking about his own prayer here. But now I wonder if he meant the father's.

Meditation: Seven-year-old William wrote to Pope Francis: "If you could do one miracle, what would it be?" Pope Francis wrote back: "Dear William, I would heal children. I've never been able to understand why children suffer. It's a mystery to me. I don't have an explanation." All human suffering, especially the suffering of children, will remain a mystery to us. But healing stories like this one remind us that in the face of that suffering, Jesus is raptly attentive.

Prayer: Jesus, you know every need of the children and loved ones we bring to you. We believe you can help us. Help our unbelief!

Jesus Heals Bartimaeus

Mark 10:46-52

⁴⁶They came to Jericho. As he and his disciples and a large crowd were leaving Jericho, Bartimaeus son of Timaeus, a blind beggar, was sitting by the roadside. ⁴⁷When he heard that it was Jesus of Nazareth, he began to shout out and say, "Jesus, Son of David, have mercy on me!" ⁴⁸Many sternly ordered him to be quiet, but he cried out even more loudly, "Son of David, have mercy on me!" ⁴⁹Jesus stood still and said, "Call him here." And they called the blind man, saying to him, "Take heart; get up, he is calling you." ⁵⁰So throwing off his cloak, he sprang up and came to Jesus. ⁵¹Then Jesus said to him, "What do you want me to do for you?" The blind man said to him, "My teacher, let me see again." ⁵²Jesus said to him, "Go; your faith has made you well." Immediately he regained his sight and followed him on the way.

32

Make Some Noise

While the healing of Jairus's daughter reminds us of the importance of silence, this story may serve as a bit of a corrective. Because sometimes it's okay to make a little noise. In Bartimaeus's case, that included a good deal of shouting.

We don't get to know most of the people who are healed by Jesus. Many of them are nameless, and some of them never speak a word. But in just seven verses, I'd say we get a pretty clear picture of Bartimaeus, son of Timaeus. This man was plucky! He had guts.

Here's Bartimaeus, described a bit insensitively as "a blind beggar" (I imagine he was used to it), sitting by the side of the road as he was wont to do. It was a logical place for a beggar to be. But on this day, Bartimaeus heard that Jesus of Nazareth was passing by. *Passing by . . .* In other words, Bartimaeus knew he had just one chance. And darn it if anyone was going to stop him from taking it.

So he began to shout. Here's where you have to admire the noisemaking. Bartimaeus would have found it difficult to jostle through a crowd, or climb a tree to rise above the throngs, or throw himself at Jesus' feet. I believe if he could have done those things, he would have—he certainly had the spirit for all of it. But given the fast-moving crowds and the apparent lack of personal support, Bartimaeus was unlikely to find his way to Jesus quickly enough on his own. So he used what he had—and apparently he had quite a loud voice. And some wits about him as well, for Bartimaeus doesn't just shout, "Help me!" He formulates a gorgeous and intentional prayer, one that has been repeated millions upon millions of times by believers in every age: "Jesus, Son of David, have mercy on me!"

Of course, Bartimaeus is immediately shushed—and not by folks who are seeking a golden moment of healing silence. No, we get the sense that they shush him because they find him annoying. They speak to him "sternly." But our man Bartimaeus is entirely undeterred; he only shouts the louder: "Son of David, have mercy on me!"

Despite everyone else's determination to shut Bartimaeus up, Jesus, who is indeed passing by, stands still for a moment and listens. He hears that piercing call, the sound of gutsy determination, faith that was growing by decibels. This man was asking for mercy. There was no way Jesus was going to pass *that* by. "Call him here," Jesus says.

The very people who had shushed Bartimaeus now tell him to get himself over to Jesus. And here's my favorite part (it's so Bartimaeus)—he doesn't just get up and go.

No, he *springs up* and throws off his cloak! That's the spirit, Bartimaeus! This is your moment!

And indeed it is. Jesus asks him what he wants—he knows Bartimaeus will speak his mind. And again, this spirited man says something so beautiful it could be liturgy: "My teacher, let me see again." In true Markan fashion, the healing is immediate.

What will Bartimaeus do now—now that life has changed dramatically, thanks to his ability to make some noise? We'd expect nothing less of Bartimaeus: he begins to follow Jesus on the way.

I wonder what happened to Bartimaeus as the weeks and months unfolded. How long did he walk with Jesus? Did he follow him all the way to Jerusalem? Was he always known as one of the pluckier members of the community?

I like to believe all those things. I imagine him sometimes breaking the golden silence, much to the dismay of his brothers and sisters. And I imagine him reminding them that sometimes it's okay, and sometimes it's holy, to make a little noise.

Meditation: The prayer of Bartimaeus, adapted slightly, is now known as the Jesus Prayer: *Lord Jesus Christ, Son of God, have mercy on me, a sinner.* Any variation of this prayer is still the Jesus Prayer. How do you pray for Jesus' mercy as he is passing by?

Prayer: Jesus, Son of David, have mercy on me!

Jesus Heals Ten Men with Leprosy

Luke 17:11-19

[11]On the way to Jerusalem Jesus was going through the region between Samaria and Galilee. [12]As he entered a village, ten lepers approached him. Keeping their distance, [13]they called out, saying, "Jesus, Master, have mercy on us!" [14]When he saw them, he said to them, "Go and show yourselves to the priests." And as they went, they were made clean. [15]Then one of them, when he saw that he was healed, turned back, praising God with a loud voice. [16]He prostrated himself at Jesus' feet and thanked him. And he was a Samaritan. [17]Then Jesus asked, "Were not ten made clean? But the other nine, where are they? [18]Was none of them found to return and give praise to God except this foreigner?" [19]Then he said to him, "Get up and go on your way; your faith has made you well."

33

Total Praise

In 1996, Gospel artist Richard Smallwood was struggling. His mother had been diagnosed with dementia, and a close friend was dying of cancer. He wanted to write a song that tapped into his pain, what he later described as a "pity-party song." But instead, he wrote the matchless anthem "Total Praise." Reminiscent of Psalm 121, "Total Praise" has since inspired millions of believers to lift their eyes to the hills and their hands to God—in *total praise*—no matter their circumstances.

The ten men in this story had every reason to thank God. They had been through a terrible ordeal—a serious illness, a separation from their community, a sense of shame—but they asked for mercy from the healer who was passing by, and immediately they were healed. It is shocking to us that only one of them "turned back" to praise God and thank Jesus. We're quick to ask with him, "Were not ten made clean? But the other nine, where are they?" This is basic. It's Gratitude 101.

But what about Richard Smallwood? What about those who do not witness or experience healing, those who have every reason to despair but instead feel something rise up within them—an urge, a Spirit, a melody—those who have not experienced the healing they yearn for but still lift their eyes to the hills and their hands in praise?

Nine men were healed and went silently on their way. One man was healed and praised God with a loud voice. But what about the hundreds (thousands?) in the region between Samaria and Galilee who were not healed that day? Did they still praise God?

Do we?

Smallwood's "Total Praise" ends with a dizzying torrent of *amens*—building and scaffolding, repeating and encoring, until choirs are utterly spent by the effort required to sing and sustain them. This kind of praise, this kind of *amen*, is the most difficult, the most exhausting, the most exhilarating, and the most sacred. This is praise born not from being healed but from being loved. It emerges from a place of deep trust and lived experience. It clings to and leans on and sings out God's promises—even as we lift our eyes, even as the sun sets across the hills.

Meditation: The lyrics of Richard Smallwood's praise anthem are simple and can be learned by heart. Search online for "Total Praise" and listen to several choirs sing it. Commit part of the song to memory so you can rely on it in times of gratitude and times of struggle.

Prayer: Loving God, no matter what happens, I lift my hands and praise you.

Jesus Heals a Man Born Blind

John 9:1-7

[1]As he walked along, he saw a man blind from birth. [2]His disciples asked him, "Rabbi, who sinned, this man or his parents, that he was born blind?" [3]Jesus answered, "Neither this man nor his parents sinned; he was born blind so that God's works might be revealed in him. [4]We must work the works of him who sent me while it is day; night is coming when no one can work. [5]As long as I am in the world, I am the light of the world." [6]When he had said this, he spat on the ground and made mud with the saliva and spread the mud on the man's eyes, [7]saying to him, "Go, wash in the pool of Siloam" (which means Sent). Then he went and washed and came back able to see.

34

Mud and Spit

I wonder what Jesus' mother would have said, had she been there to see him making mud out of dirt and spit. It might have reminded her of his childhood—surely there were some messy days after a heavy rain when Jesus, like any child, played in the mud.

But on this day, mud is serious business. It is part of the "work" Jesus is doing—work he describes with a bit of mystery: "We must work the works of him who sent me while it is day." Mud and spit—the very work of God.

John's Gospel is no stranger to symbolism, nor is it shy about evoking the ancient book of Genesis. And no doubt some readers hear in this healing story echoes of the earliest work of God—creation: "Then the LORD God formed man from the dust of the ground, and breathed into his nostrils the breath of life; and the man became a living being" (Gen 2:7). God, gathering dust and dirt and breath, mixing it all, and creating something living. Jesus does this work now, creating something new, restoring something ancient—humankind (*adam*)—from the earth (*adamah*).

We may find it confusing, even problematic, that Jesus explains this man's lifelong blindness by telling his disciples that the man "was born blind so that God's works might be revealed in him." We mustn't interpret this to mean that people suffer for the sake of God's glory. Rather, suffering is a reality of the human body and of human living. It is not the fault of the suffering person or his family (a point Jesus insists upon). And it is certainly not the desire of God, as the healing ministry of Jesus gives witness. But Jesus' observation is, at its heart, a recognition that *God does work* within the medium of human suffering—in all its mud and muck. Like a masterful creator, or a child after a rainstorm, God can make or imagine or restore beautiful things from what appears to us to be a mess.

Not just anyone could say those words. I couldn't and wouldn't say them. But Jesus can. For when he smears that mud and spit on this man's face and eyes—eyes that see for the first time, see the face of Jesus—he is already a man walking toward Jerusalem, a man who will be stripped naked, beaten, and crucified. And out of *that* dark mud and muck, the Light of the World will still shine, and God's works will be revealed.

Human suffering is not God's sandbox. It isn't a place where God plays or experiments. But it is a place where God lives and participates, a place where, for now, the mud is still being mixed and spread, where creation is still happening.

We must remember this when our eyes are opened. For we are seeing the one who knows all about spit and mud, and can even heal us with it.

Meditation: The *why* of human suffering is not easily answered, though goodness knows we've all tried. This story, like so many others, directs us away from the *why* straight to the *who*. At some point our questions about suffering must give way to a relationship. Pithy answers or even sound doctrine are unlikely to satisfy us completely. But the love of God in Christ Jesus just might (Rom 8:39).

Prayer: Jesus, Healer, I do not always understand my situation. But I trust you and your promises. Reveal the work of God in me.

Jesus and Zacchaeus

Luke 19:1-9

[1]He entered Jericho and was passing through it. [2]A man was there named Zacchaeus; he was a chief tax collector and was rich. [3]He was trying to see who Jesus was, but on account of the crowd he could not, because he was short in stature. [4]So he ran ahead and climbed a sycamore tree to see him, because he was going to pass that way. [5]When Jesus came to the place, he looked up and said to him, "Zacchaeus, hurry and come down; for I must stay at your house today." [6]So he hurried down and was happy to welcome him. [7]All who saw it began to grumble and said, "He has gone to be the guest of one who is a sinner." [8]Zacchaeus stood there and said to the Lord, "Look, half of my possessions, Lord, I will give to the poor; and if I have defrauded anyone of anything, I will pay back four times as much." [9]Then Jesus said to him, "Today salvation has come to this house."

35

Zaccheus, Come Down

One of the most profound healing stories in the Gospels is the tale of Zaccheus, the climber of sycamores. It first captured my attention as a child who loved to climb trees. The massive magnolia outside my bedroom window gave me a view of the whole neighborhood when I climbed to the top.

Zaccheus was a tax collector—a *chief* tax collector—who was collecting taxes from the Jewish people on behalf of the Roman government. Of course, this meant that Zaccheus was not very popular with his own people. His livelihood depended not only on working for the oppressor —the Roman Empire—but on charging and collecting extra, which he got to keep. Luke tells us Zaccheus was wealthy, so he must have been doing a brisk tax-collecting (and tax-embellishing) business.

Zaccheus lived in Jericho, and he heard that Jesus was coming. There was buzz about Jesus in the region—that he was a preacher who spoke with authority, that he was a wonder-worker. Things were *different* when he was around. And so, naturally, Zaccheus "was trying to see who Jesus was."

This is where we are told that Zaccheus was short in stature and that he couldn't see Jesus because of the crowd. What do short people do in a crowd? We move to higher ground. That's what Zaccheus did, of course. He climbed a tree so he could see Jesus for himself.

As Luke tells it, Jesus was just passing through town. But then he caught sight of Zaccheus in the tree. And he approached the sycamore tree and spoke words that would change Zaccheus's life forever: "Zaccheus, hurry and come down . . . I must stay at your house today."

And then, while the crowd moped and grumbled that Jesus was spending time with a sinner, Zaccheus promised to give half of all he had to the poor and to repay everyone he had ever defrauded . . . *fourfold*.

Zaccheus must not have had much left by the time he made reparation. And we can safely assume that as morning broke the next day, Zaccheus was looking for a new job. So there were some practical challenges to this new way of life. And yet, there was a lightness about Zaccheus, in his self-emptying and his starting over. Salvation—the greatest of all healings—had come to his house.

Meditation: The simplicity of this beautiful story speaks volumes about the person of Jesus. Although there was certainly more conversation between Jesus and Zaccheus than we read here, the way the story is told makes it clear that simply being in Jesus' presence, being noticed by Jesus, changed Zacchaeus forever. This was a total healing by presence, by encounter. There is no correction or chastisement. Jesus simply says to Zacchaeus, *I want to be with you today.*

Prayer: Lord Jesus, let me experience the healing of encounter so I too may be inspired to set things right, so I too may know the joy of salvation.

The Death of Lazarus

John 11:1-6, 17-21, 32-37

¹Now a certain man was ill, Lazarus of Bethany, the village of Mary and her sister Martha. ²Mary was the one who anointed the Lord with perfume and wiped his feet with her hair; her brother Lazarus was ill. ³So the sisters sent a message to Jesus, "Lord, he whom you love is ill." ⁴But when Jesus heard it, he said, "This illness does not lead to death; rather it is for God's glory, so that the Son of God may be glorified through it." ⁵Accordingly, though Jesus loved Martha and her sister and Lazarus, ⁶after having heard that Lazarus was ill, he stayed two days longer in the place where he was. . . .

¹⁷When Jesus arrived, he found that Lazarus had already been in the tomb four days. ¹⁸Now Bethany was near Jerusalem, some two miles away, ¹⁹and many of the Jews had come to Martha and Mary to console them about their brother. ²⁰When Martha heard that Jesus was coming, she went and met him, while Mary stayed at home. ²¹Martha

said to Jesus, "Lord, if you had been here, my brother would not have died. . . ."

³²When Mary came where Jesus was and saw him, she knelt at his feet and said to him, "Lord, if you had been here, my brother would not have died." ³³When Jesus saw her weeping, and the Jews who came with her also weeping, he was greatly disturbed in spirit and deeply moved. ³⁴He said, "Where have you laid him?" They said to him, "Lord, come and see." ³⁵Jesus began to weep. ³⁶So the Jews said, "See how he loved him!" ³⁷But some of them said, "Could not he who opened the eyes of the blind man have kept this man from dying?"

36

Fleeting and Forever

Most healing stories in the Gospels are brief, but the story of Jesus raising Lazarus from the dead is positively epic, its forty-four verses describing Jesus' decision to travel from across the Jordan back into Judea to "awaken" Lazarus (John 11:11), his conversations with Lazarus's sisters, and the raising itself—all of it a masterful account of illness, death, grief, friendship, and love.

On one level, the story feels complicated. (Only a portion of it is excerpted here and in the next reflection; do read the full account of John 11:1-44 if you can.) Jesus knows that Lazarus, who is described as the one Jesus loves, is ill, yet he delays going to him for two full days. He tells his disciples that he will wake Lazarus, but they confuse his death for sleep. When Jesus arrives, the sisters essentially tell Jesus that his delay has cost Lazarus his life; nevertheless, they express faith in him. And Jesus, though he has already indicated that he will wake Lazarus from death, is clearly disturbed by the grief of Mary and Martha and by

the death of his beloved friend. Those who see Jesus weeping are touched by his love, but they wonder, "Could not he
who opened the eyes of the blind man have kept this man
from dying?" We wonder the same thing. What is Jesus
doing? Is he playing games with a man's life for the sake of
inspiring faith in others? Complicated indeed!

But on another level, this story is utterly simple—and
so intimately familiar that we're sure we've lived it: God
delays, and we don't know why. God is present but isn't
fixing everything. God weeps with us, also disturbed by
death. So often, this is the pattern of illness and death, the
familiar texture of grief.

Of course, in the end Jesus does awaken Lazarus from
death, so this story has a neater ending than some of our
own. But Lazarus will die again. The resuscitation of Jesus'
friend is spectacular and miraculous, but it isn't permanent.
The only thing permanent here is the glimmer we see of
the resurrection of Jesus, the one thing that can make sense
of divine delay, the harsh reality of death, and the kind of
grief that seeps into our bones. Every physical healing—or
lack thereof—is, in a sense, fleeting. It only points to what
will be forever—the final unbinding of death (John 11:44),
the decisive defeat of its sting (1 Cor 15:55), and the wiping
away of the last tear (Rev 21:4).

Meditation: The petition of the sisters of Lazarus—*Lord,
the one you love is ill*—is a beautifully formulated prayer
that we too can use. Praying for those who are ill is a re-

sponsibility and a privilege. It isn't that God needs to be reminded, but prayer is a way to join in God's healing work. We might also use imaginative prayer to enter into this work. Imagine Jesus the Healer with your friend or loved one, extending his hand over them in the place they need healing most—their hearts or heads, the location of their cancer, or their whole bodies.

Prayer: Lord Jesus, we entrust to you all who are sick and suffering—those we love, those you love. Do not delay, but give them some share in your resurrection.

Jesus Raises Lazarus from the Dead

John 11:38-44

[38]Then Jesus, again greatly disturbed, came to the tomb. It was a cave, and a stone was lying against it. [39]Jesus said, "Take away the stone." Martha, the sister of the dead man, said to him, "Lord, already there is a stench because he has been dead four days." [40]Jesus said to her, "Did I not tell you that if you believed, you would see the glory of God?" [41]So they took away the stone. And Jesus looked upward and said, "Father, I thank you for having heard me. [42]I knew that you always hear me, but I have said this for the sake of the crowd standing here, so that they may believe that you sent me." [43]When he had said this, he cried with a loud voice, "Lazarus, come out!" [44]The dead man came out, his hands and feet bound with strips of cloth, and his face wrapped in a cloth. Jesus said to them, "Unbind him, and let him go."

37

Unbound

Here we have the ending of John's epic story of the raising of Lazarus. It's the ending we want for every death. What we wouldn't give to have our loved ones restored to us as Lazarus was to his sisters!

When my grandmother was dying, she asked me if I thought it was harder to be born or to die. Both are hard. And both are sacred. Even though death disturbs us (it disturbed Jesus, here at the tomb of Lazarus and in the Garden of Gethsemane as he faced his own), it is a rebirth. As infants in the womb, we could not imagine what was coming next. So it is for the rebirth that is death.

There's an unbinding in death, a removal of all the things that have held us back. The confines of the womb, though they feel so comforting at the time, are not where we are meant to stay. There will come a time to hear the voice of Jesus calling our names, too, calling us out of dark, confining spaces with a commanding shout. "Unbind him," Jesus said of Lazarus, "and let him go."

Could death itself be a kind of healing? I imagine that the moment babies find their way into their mothers' arms for the first time, they feel healed and whole in a way they need beyond all else. Isn't this what makes death sacred—the encounter that lies beyond the unbinding?

The first thing Lazarus must have seen was the face of Jesus, looking tired but exhilarated. And the embrace that followed? Like the moment after a birth—hard-earned, joyful and free, sacred, beautiful, and eternal.

Meditation: In speaking of the natural cycles of human life, artist, woodworker, and farmer Jack Baumgartner remarked, "It's not the wheel of life, but the wheel of life and death. It wouldn't turn without death." Death can feel abrupt and final, like an ending. How can we become better at understanding death as making the wheel turn, a dynamic that moves us into life?

Prayer: Jesus, call us out of every confining space into your eternal embrace.

Jesus Heals the Ear of the Slave of the High Priest

Luke 22:47-51

[47]While he was still speaking, suddenly a crowd came, and the one called Judas, one of the twelve, was leading them. He approached Jesus to kiss him; [48]but Jesus said to him, "Judas, is it with a kiss that you are betraying the Son of Man?" [49]When those who were around him saw what was coming, they asked, "Lord, should we strike with the sword?" [50]Then one of them struck the slave of the high priest and cut off his right ear. [51]But Jesus said, "No more of this!" And he touched his ear and healed him.

38

Wounds

Only Luke's account of Jesus' arrest in the garden includes this healing story, the last physical healing of Jesus' earthly life. It is a profound commentary on the compassion of Jesus—so innate was it, so habitual, that even in a moment of hostility and personal crisis, Jesus heals. It must have felt good to see his followers rush to his defense with such passion! But Jesus wanted nothing to do with violence.

This account presents us with an important contrast. On one hand, we witness the apparent ease with which Jesus heals the ear of the slave of the high priest. On the other, we are confronted by the difficult, deep healing that is now needed between Jesus and Judas. We know Judas's story; we're accustomed to thinking of him as the betrayer. But for years of travel and ministry, it was not so. He was a trusted companion, a member of Jesus' inner circle. *He approached Jesus to kiss him.* Betrayal by a friend cuts deep.

In this moment of crisis, we come face-to-face one last time with the distinction between being cured and being healed. The slave of the high priest is cured instantly by the touch of Jesus. This kind of healing should not be discounted. To lose an ear would have been devastating and painful. It might have exposed this man to ridicule, infection, and lifelong hearing issues. So this healing is real and significant. And yet, it was a surface wound.

The wound that has now been cut between Jesus and Judas runs much deeper. And as we know, relationships are not typically healed in an instant. They require more of everything—more time, more compassion, more vulnerability. The physical healing of an ear was essentially one-sided—Jesus was the sole agent of the healing. But the healing of relationships rarely works that way. Both people must work hard.

Luke's Gospel doesn't mention it, but Matthew's does: Judas kills himself when he discovers that Jesus has been condemned to death (Matt 27:5). A sign of how broken he was inside, beneath the surface, where wounds are harder to see and heal.

There is simply no doubt that Jesus would have healed this wound if he could have—so much did he love Judas, so willing and determined was he to heal. But this kind of healing depends not only on the healer but on the wounded. It requires us to invite, or at least allow, the healer in. To do so can be painful. It requires exposing the wound and letting the healer touch it.

Jesus, Healer, cure our surface wounds, and heal our deep ones.

Meditation: Artist Nicholas Mynheer's painting entitled "Mary Embraces Judas' Mother" is a creative interpretation of a powerful moment that is not found in Scripture but may well have happened. In the background of the painting, Jesus hangs on a cross, and Judas from a tree. In the foreground, their mothers embrace. The scene is painful, intimate, and tender, which is often the way with the healing of relationships. Wounds this deep can only be healed by love.

Prayer: Jesus, when my relationships are wounded, teach me to be a healer. Teach me to heal and be healed by love.

Jesus and Thomas

John 20:24-28

[24]But Thomas (who was called the Twin), one of the twelve, was not with them when Jesus came. [25]So the other disciples told him, "We have seen the Lord." But he said to them, "Unless I see the mark of the nails in his hands, and put my finger in the mark of the nails and my hand in his side, I will not believe."

[26]A week later his disciples were again in the house, and Thomas was with them. Although the doors were shut, Jesus came and stood among them and said, "Peace be with you." [27]Then he said to Thomas, "Put your finger here and see my hands. Reach out your hand and put it in my side. Do not doubt but believe." [28]Thomas answered him, "My Lord and my God!"

39

I Will Not Believe

Here's a different kind of healing story. It may be the one we relate to most.

Poor Doubting Thomas! That nickname, that iconic doubt! I've always sympathized with Thomas, and I've never blamed him. Believing a dead person was alive again? Of course it seemed too good to be true. But one day, hearing this Gospel proclaimed, it occurred to me: he didn't have to dig his heels in *quite* so much.

Jesus had been raised from the dead, and he appeared to his disciples. He showed them his hands and his side—proof that the crucified Lord was among them. He breathed the Spirit on them and wished them peace, and the disciples "rejoiced" (John 20:19-23). Unfortunately, Thomas was not present. Not his fault—he was probably buying food for everyone else! But geography matters. He simply wasn't there.

I'm still very much with Thomas at this point in the story. He feels confused, left out, shocked, uncertain. He's hearing exactly what he wants to hear—that Jesus lives—so of course his natural inclination is to take it with a grain of salt. It would be almost irresponsible to believe such a thing! And yet . . . *all* the other disciples say to him quite plainly, "We have seen the Lord." They don't sound hysterical in the least. But I can still understand Thomas's uncertainty. I too would be slow to come around.

But now we come to Thomas's response. He answers so quickly, so firmly, so defiantly: "Unless I see the mark of the nails in his hands, and put my finger in the mark of the nails and my hand in his side . . ." Three conditions for faith; three things that have to happen just so; three ways of limiting himself, his imagination, his experiences. And if the conditions aren't met? "I will not believe," he says.

It's a shame to miss out on so much.

What's surprising in the story is that Jesus doesn't mind. He comes back a week later, and we get the sense that it's Thomas he comes for. With one beautiful greeting, he invites Thomas to do it all—to see his hands, to touch his wounds, to believe. "Reach out your hand," Jesus says. This is a healing story after all.

I like to think that when Jesus was healing someone, he wasn't thinking about anyone else. Whether a result of divine compassion or of incredible human focus, I believe everyone else fell away, and in those moments, there were only two. And here were Jesus and Thomas in the Upper Room, totally focused on each other. That kind of focus always heals.

We've all been the doubter in the room. Doubt is natural, but there's no reason to dig our heels in, to miss out on what God is accomplishing. We may have trouble thinking big, or thinking beyond, or dreaming, or imagining. But as long as we don't refuse, there will always be time to stretch out our hands, to touch the compassionate heart of the risen healer, to believe and say with the faith of Thomas, "My Lord and my God!" This is the first and only time, by the way, that Jesus is directly addressed as "God" in the Gospels.

This story isn't just about healing from doubt. It is about healing from every way we limit ourselves, every way we stop short of experiencing the sacred, every way we've learned to say, "I will not believe." It is healing from our refusal to encounter life, resurrection, *egeiro*. It is healing from our refusal to be changed.

Meditation: This encounter between Thomas and the risen Christ (so beautifully portrayed by Jack Baumgartner on the cover of this book) may expand our understanding of Jesus' healing ministry as reaching deep within us, even into our long-held patterns of thinking. Doubt, worry, discontent, resentment—as long as we don't dig our heels in, as long as we leave Jesus just a bit of space to work, he can heal us. Remember his encouraging words to Thomas, which he says to us, too: "Reach out" and "believe."

Prayer: Jesus—my Lord and my God—when I doubt, when I set conditions, when I dig my heels in, heal me.

The Judgment of the Nations

Matthew 25:34-40

[34]"Then the king will say to those at his right hand, 'Come, you that are blessed by my Father, inherit the kingdom prepared for you from the foundation of the world; [35]for I was hungry and you gave me food, I was thirsty and you gave me something to drink, I was a stranger and you welcomed me, [36]I was naked and you gave me clothing, I was sick and you took care of me, I was in prison and you visited me.' [37]Then the righteous will answer him, 'Lord, when was it that we saw you hungry and gave you food, or thirsty and gave you something to drink? [38]And when was it that we saw you a stranger and welcomed you, or naked and gave you clothing? [39]And when was it that we saw you sick or in prison and visited you?' [40]And the king will answer them, 'Truly I tell you, just as you did it to one of the least of these who are members of my family, you did it to me.'"

40

We Are Healers, Too

If gathering so many healing stories from the Gospels into one place tells us anything, it's that healing was not just an occasional occurrence in the ministry of Jesus. It isn't something he did when he had time, or when he came across an especially sad situation, or when healing would garner a particular response. It is something he did *all the time*. It is part of who he was.

Jesus was also a masterful preacher and our savior. But healing was a centerpiece of his life and ministry—it demonstrated what the preaching was about, it pointed to both the cross and the resurrection.

Jesus gathered disciples about him, great numbers of disciples (Luke 6:17). And *all of them* were called to follow him (9:23). Following him was literal for a time—they needed to be with him and pay attention. But once Jesus was gone, they followed him by doing his work.

This era has not come to an end. It is we who continue it. The healing ministry of Jesus is alive and well among family members, caregivers, chaplains, medical professionals, counselors, ministers, friends, strangers, those who accompany the hurting and the dying—and among all human beings who find within themselves a reservoir of compassion and a hand that stretches out to the other.

St. John of the Cross wrote, "In the evening of life, we shall be judged on our love." Yes, we will be judged on how well we cared for one another—whether we were present, whether we noticed, whether we could be silent and whether we could make some noise, whether we were vulnerable, whether we forgave, whether we stretched, and whether we healed.

Our reservoir may not be as deep as that of Jesus. When sunset comes around, we may be exhausted; healing a crowd may be beyond our capability or even our imagination. But we will find our own ways to carry on the healing ministry of Jesus.

Because we are healers, too.

Meditation:
Christ has no body but yours,
No hands, no feet on earth but yours,
Yours are the eyes with which he looks
Compassion on this world,
Yours are the feet with which he walks to do good,
Yours are the hands with which he blesses all the world.
Yours are the hands, yours are the feet,
Yours are the eyes, you are his body.

Christ has no body now but yours.

—Attributed to St. Teresa of Avila

Prayer: Jesus, may I look on this world with your compassion. May I stretch out my hands with your love.

Acknowledgments

I am grateful to my colleagues at Liturgical Press, who skillfully turn words into books and share them with others. *Thank you*. Special thanks to Hans Christoffersen, whose encouragement I needed to move forward with this book and whose support as a colleague and friend has blessed me.

I am thankful to those who provided feedback on this manuscript before publication: my husband, Ono, always my first reader and a healing presence in my life every day; my mom, Ruth Vineyard, who wears many hats as mothers do, including proofreader and encourager; Tom Stegman's sister, Patricia Hasty, a good friend who knows a great deal about healing; and Mahri Leonard-Fleckman, whose biblical expertise and friendship have enriched this book and my life.

And with hands outstretched, I give thanks for all who have been a gentle presence in my life, who make real for me the healing ministry of Jesus.

References

3. The Holy One of God
Amy-Jill Levine, *Signs and Wonders: A Beginner's Guide to the Miracles of Jesus* (Nashville: Abingdon Press, 2022), xvii.

13. Pot of Gold
Pope Francis, Angelus at St. Peter's Square, Vatican City, February 14, 2021, https://www.vatican.va/content/francesco/en/angelus/2021/documents/papa-francesco_angelus_20210214.html.

31. A Parent's Prayer
Pope Francis, *Dear Pope Francis: The Pope Answers Questions from Children Around the World* (Chicago: Loyola Press, 2016).

37. Unbound
Artful, season 3, episode 6, "Sunny Taylor / Jack Baumgartner," aired October 16, 2022, on BYUtv.

38. Wounds
Nicholas Mynheer, "Mary Embraces Judas' Mother," from The Life of Mary series, 2014, oil on paper, 20cm x 20cm, https://www.mynheer-art.co.uk/gallery/paintings.html.

40. We Are Healers, Too

St. John of the Cross, *Dichos* 64, quoted in the *Catechism of the Catholic Church*, 2nd ed. (United States Catholic Conference—Libreria Editrice Vaticana, 1997), paragraph 1022.

The poem "Christ Has No Body" is traditionally attributed to St. Teresa of Avila but is not found in her published works. Accessed at https://www.journeywithjesus.net/poemsand prayers/3637-Teresa_Of_Avila_Christ_Has_No_Body.